W9-BND-422

Ethics for Fundraisers

Philanthropic Studies

ROBERT L. PAYTON AND DWIGHT F. BURLINGAME
General Editors

Ethics
for Fundraisers

ALBERT ANDERSON

Indiana University Press

BLOOMINGTON AND INDIANAPOLIS

The paper used in this publication meets the minimum require-
ments of American National Standard for Information Sciences—
Permanence of Paper for Printed Library Materials,
ANSI Z39.48-1984.

Manufactured in the United States of America

Library of Congress Cataloging-in-Publication Data

Anderson, Albert, date
  Ethics for fundraisers / Albert Anderson.
    p. cm.—(Philanthropic studies)
  Includes index.
  ISBN 0-253-33028-9 (cloth : alk. paper). — ISBN 0-253-21052-6
(pbk. : alk. paper)
   1. Fund raising—Moral and ethical aspects. 2. Fund raisers
(Persons)—Professional ethics. 3. Nonprofit organizations—
Finance. 4. Charities—Finance. I. Title. II. Series.
HV41.2.A53 1996
174'.9361—dc20   95-4612

1 2 3 4 5 01 00 99 98 97 96

Contents

Acknowledgments

From the beginning my intention has been to write something helpful for those who, like myself, often have difficulty discerning and defending an ethical course of action in philanthropic work. Failing that purpose I have no one to blame but myself. Where I have succeeded, it is due in considerable part to the suggestions by thoughtful and experienced persons whom I admire and respect. I am indebted particularly to Robert Payton, Dwight Burlingame, James Shannon, Kenneth Goodpaster, Sidney Rand, Eugene Tempel, Charles Mundale, Henry Rosso, Warren Smerud, Paula Parker-Sawyers, Per Anderson, Janet Huettner, Dianne Hennes, Robert Voigt, and Thor Anderson. I am no less grateful to my family: my wife, Anita, who in every sense of the word gave moral support to the effort; and our children and their spouses, who showed more than a purely filial interest in it. Without the encouragement of all, this book might never have been completed.

Introduction

This is a book in applied ethics—ethical decision-making for practitioners in the work of philanthropy: nonprofit staff and volunteers, professionals and grantmakers who play their distinctive roles in causes they are united to support in great part by raising and distributing private gifts and grants.

While the book should prove to be of value to all who are interested in philanthropy, its primary aim is to enhance the level of ethical fundraising throughout the nonprofit sector by equipping development professionals and volunteers with the frameworks for understanding and taking principled action, for preventing unethical behavior, and thus for building bridges of trust to the charitable community.

To the casual observer the book may seem out of touch with contemporary lifestyles. In a culture characterized by pervasive moral ambiguity, where just about anything not illegal goes, talk about virtue, character, and principled behavior seems oddly out of date or downright silly. Who needs it?

Unfortunately, the question is not merely colloquial. Astute observers of society suggest we have lost our traditional moral bearings. We are cast about—to defile the scriptural simile—by every wind of relativism. Where once we could rely on parental, religious, or educational doctrine to give us firm if not always palatable direction, things have changed. Moral authority is no longer what it was. Item: familial persuasion is impotent or absent when violent crime among children, who seem puzzled by questions about conscience, is growing. Unaccustomed to moral decision-making, atrophied since youth, we delegate it elsewhere. If our rights to live as we please seem threatened, the first rule is to see an attorney and rely on the law to secure them.

This moral confusion comes at a time when deciding on the right course of action seems uncommonly critical to individual and social well-being. Medical professionals need direction about the prolonging, and taking, of life; threats to the global environment are critical, but at odds with economic expansion in hard-pressed third world nations; business executives know they should be socially responsible, but find that investing in a noteworthy cause may diminish the welfare of employees and shareholders. Philanthropy has its ethical tensions, too, when the top executive of one of the nation's most important nonprofits exploits his position to enrich himself.

If I am right, the task is not that we need more ethics; that is understood. The trick is how to be responsible in a morally vacillating culture. This book addresses the issue modestly by setting out to help one sector of ethical concern: nonprofit practitioners in philanthropy, who may themselves be confused by the multiple standards of conduct and attitude they experience. They seek a lasting and consistent framework for doing the right thing more often than not. Succeeding in that I think has a lot to do with character, however archaic it sounds.

In a context of concern for social diversity and multiculturalism, where tolerance is rightly urged but not always rightly understood, the task is daunting. Fortunately, many others in nonprofit management, grantmaking, and fundraising are making similar efforts to think clearly in their own way. Interestingly, one of the things we seem to share is an admiration for the ethical insights of three standouts in the history of thought: Aristotle, Immanuel Kant, and John Stuart Mill.

The reason probably goes beyond admiration. These classic figures are not merely prominent for their influence on Western civility. As thoughtful ethicists, they probably represent at a secular level the three most compelling ways we find of thinking about ethics—ways that correspond unusually well with our deepest, but not always orderly, dispositions to do the right thing. Call it good, if not innately moral, sense. Aristotle reaffirms our sense that individual character is fundamental to the good life. In the process, he develops what it means to be morally responsible, in a way that is enduringly pertinent to those who are devoted to philanthropy. Kant elicits our sense of ideal self-respect, and identifies morally worthy action with what is rationally imperative regardless of one's temptations to do otherwise. And Mill, opposing Kant, presents the pervasive and naturally sensible view that doing whatever is more beneficial than harmful for the most people is doing the right thing.

If indeed we resonate even now to what these writers from another time say we ought to consider, then it is never out of date to do the right thing. And if one seeks to be ethically responsible, it is hard to avoid them. The task for practitioners—the task to which this book is dedicated—is to know what it is to do the right thing and to do it. While most practitioners have good moral instincts, they have no confidence that what they feel they ought to do will stand up to the scrutiny of a culture that would resist their conviction by espousing the rightness of virtually any alternative moral or quasi-moral opinion.

Sadly, some contemporary ethicists who understand the time-honored theorists well are not very helpful. From their work in academic circles they presume, with some justification, that ethical theories are too complex or too much at odds with one another for the average practitioner to appreciate, or more likely, to *want* to appreciate. They tend to confine their insights to the classroom and to professional journals for audiences *prepared to understand them*. As occasional consultants to nonprofit associations, they underestimate practitioners who are eager to learn and apply the theory, by suggesting that doing the right thing is pretty much a personal thing, a judgment call, since no one formula is free of flaws and acceptable to all.

This book is presumptuous in its own right. Learning what it is to do the right thing by applying what the theorists seem to say to the practice of philanthropy is not easy, but neither is it hopeless. If one is looking for a book on ethical self-improvement in ten easy steps, this is not it. One will find—particularly in the first two chapters—that what it means to think and act in an ethically responsible way is challenging stuff, likely to elicit more questions than answers. True, there are ample practical examples and cases of applied theory along the way; and the treatment of ethical frameworks that take their character from Kant and Mill aims only at their practical essence. But if ethics were made to look as simple as the syndicated columns on sex and human relationships, it would only contribute to the moral ambiguity we already experience.

It is simply the nature of ethics, unlike arithmetic, to be uncertain. Its issues, choices, and actions can provoke head-shaking, demand thoughtfulness, consistency, and decisiveness—with no clear or certain prospect that one's decision is wholly right. In that respect doing ethics can benefit from a certain amount of structure, a kind of discipline guided by durable principles. However, given the mysteries of the human condition, and the often perplexing nature of day-to-day experience, being ethically responsible also demands moral imagination and resourcefulness. In a word, it takes artfulness—provided it entails no mortal blow to consistency or leads to an act of hypocrisy.

Is it worth the effort? Moral *expediency* makes no such demands. But if the old-fashioned ethicists are right, well-being—yours, mine, the organization's, society's—is at stake. One thing I can promise: the practitioner who persists in understanding the ethical ideas and issues that follow will be better equipped than before to decide and to do the right thing.

Briefly, here is what I will do:

Invoking a few classic sources for their enduring and therefore contemporary value, I begin in chapter 1 with Aristotle's notions of virtuous character and beneficence as perspectives for describing what ideally it means to be responsible about matters of philanthropy. I examine this model using examples from current nonprofit activity, and compare it with the Judeo-Christian ideal represented by Jesus' striking challenge to the rich and virtuous ruler.

In chapter 2, I examine what it means to think and act in an ethically justifiable manner by noting briefly what other major ethicists, mainly two, have thought. Supplanting moral relativism with consistent principles for ethical decision-making, Immanuel Kant and John Stuart Mill present two compelling but competing ethical frameworks for judging the moral worth of our actions.

The choice they offer is between what, above all, we understand our duty to be, and what will likely result in the greatest benefit.

In chapter 3, I examine the tensions of an ethical decision by considering a range of issues embedded in nonprofit and professional experience today, and note how each of the major competing frameworks might illuminate them.

Thus aware of what makes an issue ethical, I suggest in chapter 4 a process for decision-making, a set of principles for justifying one's chosen actions, and examples for applying the principles. Next follows a hypothetical case dealing with the tensions created by committed but ethically confused members and supporters of a nonprofit organization. Guidance for addressing these tensions is provided after each situation.

To cap what it is to be ethical in nonprofit work, chapter 5 considers a modest program for developing, and thereafter refining with an ongoing regimen, a code of ethics for one's organization. I offer a model with sample provisions that encompass a code's essential elements. The chapter concludes with a review of the overall case for doing the right thing.

Ethics for Fundraisers

One   *A Question of Responsibility*

> To give away money is an easy matter, and in any man's power.
> But to decide to whom to give it, and how large, and when, and
> for what purpose is neither in every person's power nor an easy
> matter.
>
> —Aristotle (384–322 B.C.)

Nonprofit staff members, volunteer leaders, and foundation grantmakers alike adorn their desks with this paraphrase from Aristotle's classic *Nichomachean Ethics*.[1] Joined with donors in a symbi-
otic association for society's good, each no doubt has reason to
find this ancient but enduring insight meaningful.

Professional fundraisers supported by committed volunteers
seek an elusive combination of timing and incentive that turns a
prospect into a satisfied donor. Those with charitable intent hope
their contributions, large or small, are efficiently and effectively
used. Grantmakers try to discern the worthiest purposes among
the many qualified nonprofits that need their limited funds. And
each has a unique and often difficult role to play in the ongoing
drama we call American philanthropy.[2]

What we all have in common is a responsibility to play our
roles well. For nonprofit practitioners, conscientious volunteers,
and foundation grantmakers, the concept goes to the heart of professionalism. Easy to miss, however, and a source of profound confusion, is the difference between *role* responsibility and *ethical*
responsibility—a difference that, as Aristotle suggests, is hardly
"an easy matter." The difference is important because of the
deceptively easy substitution of role-playing for truly ethical behavior.

For example, carrying out one's responsibilities as a development professional is not an easy matter. It entails the proficient ap-

plication of skills and judgment gained only with technical preparation, hard work, and experience.

As an agent of philanthropy, the professional is responsible to the donor, to represent his or her best interests in the exchange of private funds for the organization's values. At the same time, the professional is also responsible, in the company of others, to the organization, to further its mission in education, health care, the arts, religion, the environment, human needs, and other worthy causes.

Indeed, role-playing requires so much of our attention that it can displace if not replace the even more difficult task of being ethical. Like appealing to authority, it can become a crutch to relieve us of the weight of hard moral choices for matters that are not only professional but deeply personal.

Clearly, as Aristotle's *Ethics* implies, one can play a role well and still not be *ethically* responsible or accountable for one's acts, unless that role is consistent with good individual character and derived from enduring guidelines that justify one's efforts.

An example from the corporate foundation world illustrates the challenge.[3] A senior manager of the corporation, who has been approached for a grant by a close friend on a nonprofit board, asks the foundation director to give the proposal special attention. The proposal fits the foundation's grantmaking guidelines, but the nonprofit is not a good candidate for a grant, based on its performance. The director knows he ought to deny the request, but also recognizes the jeopardy to his position of crossing the senior manager, not to mention the danger of illegal "self-dealing." What is the right thing to do? The decision for the director will be hard, say the authors, and avoided only if it is understood in advance of such conflicts that the foundation's interests are independent of the corporation's, and that the firm will operate a philanthropic program reflecting standards of what is fair and proper.

As we shall see, Aristotle sets a high ethical standard for philanthropists and, by implication, their agents. However, to understand what it means to be morally accountable, not just proficient or generous, we have to begin with a familiar metaphor that has endured throughout extant history to characterize ethical decision-making. It is the picture of "drawing lines."

In an earlier time this metaphor would conjure the image of a wise old teacher who, as he introduces his students to the elements of geometry, draws a line with a stick in the sand at their feet. The line, he explains, is basic to many geometric concepts. But it also serves to separate and bound one area from another, much as the horizon separates the earth from the sky; or as a boy marks off his private domain from that of his rival by digging a furrow with his heel on the ground between them, then daring his nemesis to cross it.

These lines, this ancient sage suggests, are visible and uneven. However, the *idea* of a line, the line one sees only with the mind's eye, the definition or "real" line in geometry, is perfectly straight. This ideal line is the *standard* against which all observable, often imperfect lines are measured. The concepts of geometry describe the invisible structure of nature, the conceptual world behind the observable world.

And, adds the teacher, there is more. Consider the possibility of another, more important kind of line—call it THE LINE—that separates mortals from immortals, a standard for human beings (and even lesser gods and heroes) against which all behavior is measured. Unless we keep this LINE always in mind, we may fall prey to *hubris*, the ultimate failure, the pride that comes of wanting to be godlike—which as the great dramatists of antiquity were to show invariably leads to misfortune and tragedy. The good life, the prudent way, is a matter of drawing the right lines.

Above all, the lesson the old sage teaches is that *there are lines*—some drawn for us and some we draw ourselves—lines that also serve as limits to human behavior. Nonetheless, within the boundaries of human capacity *we are free*—a basic assumption for grounding responsibility—free not only to draw such lines but to cross over them as well.

Today as in the distant past, the image of "drawing lines" is virtually the defining paradigm for expressing ethical thought and action. Almost daily we are forced to decide where to draw the line between what we "should" and "should not" do, the language of morality.

Of course from the fact that we *do* draw lines, it doesn't necessarily follow that there *are* such lines, written into reality like laws of nature, with which our drawing attempts to conform. It may be enough to view moral decision-making as simply a matter of drawing lines.

Doubtless Aristotle was familiar with the concept, and assumed in his thinking about ethics the metaphysical conviction that there are lines written into the nature of things to which our own decisions and actions should conform. But he also seems to have improved upon another very popular and logically related epigram, as well known to the ancient Egyptian and Chinese civilizations as it was to the Greeks. It took the form "Nothing too much" or "Nothing in excess," and it too endures to this day.

It reflects the deep-seated intuition that, as experience tends to show, too much of anything is bad; and the idea is to learn *moderation* in all things. Eat too much, drink too much, exercise too much, and you'll pay for it; moderation is best. Indeed, the theme of moderation or "balance" is central to Confucianism, Zen Buddhism, and, not surprisingly, common sense.

But even without a belief that the quality of our decision-making is measured by reference to some *absolute* standard such as THE LINE, we could be seeking some *relative* standard such as moderation or balance—which, one could argue, is also a kind of absolute. Discover what it means to lead a balanced lifestyle and, according to the ancient Chinese precepts in the I *Ching*, for example, you will also find the secret to happiness; do it very well, and you will know how to be a virtuous leader among your peers.[4]

Aristotle used this image to devise a general formula for embodying truly virtuous behavior. In fact, as we shall see, his formula strengthens both metaphors by asserting that to fall short of one's potential (where the line should be drawn) is as bad as overreaching it (going over the line).

Such moral lessons, well rooted in popular culture to this day, certainly influenced Aristotle's sense of moral accountability or responsibility. However, as the father of ancient science he also taught us the need to analyze such concepts. What does "responsible action" entail?

RESPONSIBLE ACTION

Commonly, to be responsible means to be the cause, or better, the agent of some action, directly or indirectly. Responsible agency entails voluntary action, the capacity to take any of several possible courses of action. In short, to be responsible we must first be free to act.

In philanthropy, for example, to consciously initiate a gift or grant presupposes the donor's freedom of choice, without which one's action cannot, according to Aristotle, be held either praiseworthy or blameworthy. However, the fact that a donor or a fundraiser is the cause or agent of a gift is a necessary but not a sufficient condition of morally responsible action.

In a second sense of the term, to be responsible is to assume a role. We play various roles—as parents, citizens, community volunteers, professionals, each with its own job description, its own aims and expectations, its own requirements. This sense derives its force from the job to be done, the mission of the organization, or the aims of the philanthropist. As we noted, however, the actions that define a role may not be moral.

To Aristotle, neither of these senses marks a moral responsibility unless the governing purpose accords with actions embedded in virtuous character. Character is the sum of enduring dispositions, good or bad, that define the individual and are cultivated over a lifetime. The task of every human being is to develop those traits or "virtues," such as courage, beneficence, and justice, among a few others that, as experience shows, are most admired by people everywhere.

Expanding the formula for "nothing in excess," each virtue represents an admirable person's capacity to consistently discern and embody the most appropriate action, specifically one that avoids the "vicious" or vice-like extremes of "too much" (excess) and "too little" (deficiency). Using a rough geometric analogy, Aristotle describes the perfect choice as the Golden Mean.

Thus, the courageous individual, for example, is neither foolhardy (excessive) nor cowardly (deficient); weighing the risks against the stakes, the individual takes admirable action. So too, the beneficent person, while hoping to improve society through a generous gift, manages by the best choice of actions to avoid both self-aggrandizement (excessive) and penury (deficient), traits admired by no one.

Aristotle was a teleologist. He believed that like everything in the universe, we are purposive creatures whose predominant aim in life is to achieve *eudaimonia*, well-being or happiness. This is the ultimate goodness, the end for which everything else is a means. It is not, as we shall see, the simple notion that the end justifies the means, nor an ancient form of Utilitarianism, the view synonymous with John Stuart Mill (in chapter 2). Aristotle's view is simply a kind of human self-realization in which the means consistently chosen to achieve goodness are good as well.

To Aristotle, the formula of the Golden Mean is not problematic. It represents what he and his students had observed in cultures everywhere. Experience shows us that this is the way to become truly virtuous, that is, to realize one's greatest potential as a human being.

The view is self-improvement theory at its best, and the final answer to the question: Why should one be moral? Aristotle might be tempted to say that "it pays" to be artfully moderate, as common experience agrees; but not in the sense intended by those today who urge corporations to develop a code of ethics as a smart means to promote good will and greater profitability. Socrates (470–399 B.C.), who really inspired the development of moral philosophy in Greece before Aristotle, held that the unexamined life is unworthy of human beings; moral knowledge is paramount, because thinking and acting rightly builds character, which is its own reward.[5]

Thus, to the ancients, moral responsibility is a matter of character development. For Aristotle, that happens not through a solitary act of courage or justice or beneficence—say, a one-time gift of $1 million—but by a readiness *always* to act in the most virtuous or morally excellent manner. Contrary to what some donors have no doubt thought (and some fundraisers or volunteers may have encouraged), one cannot simply buy this kind of virtue.

To Aristotle, achieving moral excellence begins as a natural bent to gain happiness mainly by discovering and developing a pattern of actions shaped by self-conscious choices that draw the line between too much and too little, the excessive and the deficient—hardly, as the popular paraphrase insists, an easy matter.

The nature of the process should be underscored. To Aristotle, while being virtuous is no precise science, it is nonetheless a demanding and thoroughly rational *art*, whose mastery is vital to achieve human potential. Unfortunately, as he recognized, moral decision-making lacks the conceptual clarity and compelling certainty of Euclidean geometry.

Interestingly, only two Aristotelian virtues qualify as *ethically* essential to an excellent lifestyle: justice and (uncommon) beneficence. These two alone have moral priority over everything else that is admirable about human beings. Like other virtues, each has its characteristic requirements, but each is also governed by its own ethical motive whose end is the improvement or well-being of the individual and society.

Beneficence—"active goodness," as one dictionary defines it—is not only virtuous, it is an ethical responsibility on all fours with justice. As the *philanthropic* virtue, it exemplifies the uncommon artfulness that ethics demands. It requires that two of the abilities we most admire, namely to acquire wealth and to distribute it—each an art in its own right—be combined appropriately in one and the same personal character.

Moreover, because virtue is an enduring disposition of character and not a one-time act, beneficence reflects an ongoing pattern of admirably generous, honest, and benign behavior. As Aristotle says, that is neither in every person's power nor an easy matter.

THE GOVERNING MOTIVE FOR ACTION

For Aristotle, distinguishing and separating the ethical virtues by their governing motive is important for revealing the thoughtful purpose or intent of one's actions, that is, whether one is acting primarily for the sake of justice or beneficence or something else. Clearly, accumulated experience consistently guided by reason is the best assurance of a good result. Independently of the result, however, responsible action is a conscious, voluntary, well-intended choice, of means as well as ends.

For philanthropy, the point is somewhat shocking. To Aristotle, moral goodness cannot be judged apart from character. That the result of a grant or gift happens to be beneficial is nice. But without the unconditional "charitable intent" (to use a familiar fundraiser's phrase), out of resources honestly and benignly acquired, the act has no ethical merit.

Indeed, if a good result is the criterion of moral worth, then (as we shall see in chapter 2) the Utilitarian creed of "the greatest good for the greatest number" is sufficient. In that case Ivan Boesky, of insider-trading infamy during the 1980s, is an eminent philanthropist for the substantial gifts he made to charity, from funds he allegedly acquired through fraud.

Are fundraisers right who insist the gift—or perhaps the amount—is everything, and the source or motive behind it is of no philanthropic relevance? Their model might be the founder of the Salvation Army who reputedly said, "I would take money from the devil himself and wash it in the tears of the widows and little children." But if Aristotle is right, "dirty" money is a moral embarrassment, and neither Boesky nor the devil is a philanthropist.

Derek Bok, the former president of Harvard University, the most highly endowed nonprofit in America, once reflected in "An Open Letter" on the ethical problems of accepting gifts, including those from controversial donors.[6] He argued that it is expecting too much of an institution that receives thousands of gifts annually to pass ethical judgment on each donor. What is critical, he noted, is that accepting a gift does not by itself imply an endorsement of the views or actions of the donor; "indeed, an institution will doubtless do more good by using such funds constructively than by forcing the donor to keep his money." It may, he said, be "in bad taste" to be associated with an unsavory benefactor, but "it is doubtful that universities have an obligation to reject such gifts." However, he also insists the university would not accept a gift from one whose wealth was known to be gained by fraud. So Bok's position is confusing. Surely knowing or not knowing about the donor (and thousands of others) cannot be the difference between unethical and ethical (or non-ethical) gifts. Perhaps the issue is more complex.

For Aristotle, we have said, the person we universally admire is always drawing lines, consistently discerning and embodying behavior that is just right. Such constancy arises out of and builds on character. Together with justice (temperance)—the only other distinctively moral virtue—philanthropy (beneficence) is fundamental to human well-being. The morally excellent person will be liberally disposed, one who embodies that famous Golden Mean between the vice-prone extremes of extravagant spending and Scrooge-like parsimony.

However, we also noted that giving is only one side of it. How one acquires wealth is closely related to how one gives it away, and the rightness of governing motives is critical. For Aristotle, the idea of a well-motivated donor whose wealth is gained by consciously fraudulent or harmful means is an oxymoron.

While Aristotle does allow in his *Ethics* for harmful but blameless actions that are done involuntarily or out of ignorance, to correct those actions through charity would not qualify as true beneficence. An act must be voluntary and self-conscious to be worthy of praise or blame. Unless the governing motive is to be charitable, the act is not beneficent.

The "Model Standards of Practice for the Charitable Gift Planner," promulgated by the National Committee on Planned Giving and its members, states as its first principle the "primacy of philanthropic motivation," with the burden on the donor: "The principal basis for making a charitable gift should be a desire on the part of the donor to support the work of charitable institutions."[7] The principle is well meaning but, typical of code provisions (see chapter 5), not greatly instructive.

A case involving a private college reveals the problem.[8]

In response to a major capital gift, the recipient college publicly announced that it would name a new building after the donor.

Shortly afterward it was discovered and widely reported that for years the donor had carried out an extensive personal letter crusade, anonymously aimed at those he felt were caught up in the evils of interracial and mixed-religion marriages. Recipients of his letters, identified from public records, experienced anger, fear, and harassment. When confronted, the donor-author insisted he had meant no harm, and, based on his reading of the Old Testament, his only intention was to educate the unwary to the dangers of their new relationships.

To the chagrin of the college, a church-related, liberal arts institution, the contrast between its mission and his was stark. The college, which had already committed the funds, decided to keep the gift but remove his name from the building—conditions the donor agreed to.

Under the circumstances it may strike us as inappropriate to regard this donor as a philanthropist. Is it the gift, or the thought, that counts? For Aristotle, both the gift and the thought are important. Unfortunately, the gift of "the widow's mite" (as we shall see, below), for all its magnitude relative to her resources, will not qualify. Only a gift that measurably enhances the public good will do.

The donor's governing motive and charitable intent are paramount, Aristotle insists, because they reflect on the donor's character. Charitable intent implies that the donor is disposed above all to be beneficent and to expect nothing but perhaps a sense of well-being in return. No quid pro quo results in personal influence or economic advantage to him. It is worth noting, moreover, that charitable intent may not end with the donor. This trait can be cultivated and developed by an ethical fundraiser or recipient organization that takes care, for example, to avoid misleading or deceptive requests for funds—or the self-serving encouragement of noncharitable incentives.

Recently, an executive representing the nonprofit sector has objected to the common practice of naming facilities after major donors as a "flagrant marketing of donor recognition."[9] He cites the example of the Hirschhorn Museum, so-named for the donor who gave 6,000 works of art on the condition that the museum be named after him. To the executive, the decision demeans "the spirit of giving and the honorific value of public places." He also questions the 1993 version of the "Donor Bill of Rights"[10] provision describing the donor's right to receive "appropriate," in place of "accurate or prompt acknowledgment and recognition." The term, he suggests, "implies that donors can expect to receive commensurate recognition—the larger the gift, the greater the recognition." While the Hirschhorn condition apparently does not apply to the college donor case, veteran fundraisers often do experience the potential for demeaning "the spirit of giving" or charitable intent, in the complex and intimate dynamics of cultivating prospective major donors.

Quid pro quo arrangements can be very subtle. In recent years development professionals, and particularly those in planned giving, have couched their fundraising efforts in marketing terms. To avoid being crass, the appeal may speak of "an exchange of values" (not necessarily ethical values) that takes place between the donor and recipient organization.[11] While the concept of exchanging the donor's tangible assets for an intangible cause is very effective for promoting the relationship, it can subtly underscore the businesslike transactions—"investments" or "advantages," as promotions frequently note—that motivate or appeal to the smart consumer, well short of the single-mindedness of charitable intent.

In the case of the liberal arts college, the obvious clash with a more moderate Judeo-Christian reading of the Old Testament was not the donor's governing motive, or he would have withdrawn the gift once the difference with his own views became clear. Was it simply the educational mission of the college, the tradition of free inquiry and open debate, that moved him to give? Yet, how is it that by taking the gift the college recognized no conflict between its confessional heritage and its educational nature?

Or was the donor, based on his personal financial planning, simply sold on the prospect of substantial tax savings? While it is true that Congress has provided these tax incentives, the strategy is not lost on fundraisers either. The competition for charitable dollars prompts nonprofit organizations to more aggressively market planned gifts as prudent, wealth-conserving proposals to prospective donors.

One could argue there is no moral harm to donors who know what they are doing; whose motives are primarily financial, not charitable, having decided that the rewards outweigh the risks. But is there a moral cost to the vulnerable and less savvy, who are persuaded to give a major portion of their assets against their later, better judgment? Cynics, who say planned giving has become "planned receiving," fear the trend: one study of bequests to nonprofits reveals that an alarming number of wills are later contested, often by donors' families alleging that charities exercised inappropriate influence on the donors.[12]

To Aristotle, charitable intent is a value-added quality of philanthropy. Today, however, there are those who hold that, except for illegal or unreasonable restrictions on a gift, a donor's intentions are not relevant to the philanthropic uses of wealth. A donor, it is argued, may have multiple motives impossible to prioritize, let alone detect. Isn't it absurd, as Bok suggests, to expect nonprofit organizations such as hospitals, churches, and colleges to accept money only from the pure in heart?

Assume that the college donor, who was certainly no criminal, intended his gift as a gift, with no strings attached. Is there any reason not to regard him as a philanthropist? Perhaps only if one presses the case that he was deluded, which would, as Aristotle asserts, relieve him of culpability and thus of moral blame. On the surface, however, the donor's personal vision was not based on poor observation or faulty logic. On the contrary, he went about his educational mission self-consciously, if insensitively; he was true to his convictions. His intentions might well have been as honorable as the source of his wealth.

Yet it is difficult to avoid the judgment that the college has taken dirty money, with which philanthropy cannot afford to be associated. For example, it has been said that by accepting the gift from one of such shocking convictions the college not only is sending out messages that seem contrary to its mission, it is also "debasing public standards."

It is one thing to require that charitable wealth originate on ethical grounds. Does it also require that its recipients be ethical? The question is either silly or basic to charitable relationships, akin to the question "Why be ethical at all?" Philanthropy thrives only in an environment of trust, of mutual respect between donor and recipient, and cannot be accountable without it.

Aristotle would not likely relieve the recipient organization or fundraiser of moral responsibility. He would probably regard the advent of professional fundraisers and grantmakers as agents and champions of philanthropic virtue, representing both of its major components: rightly gaining and distributing wealth. In this more complex society, moreover, he would have expected us to be specialists in charitable intent, and to abide by morally justifiable codes which require that gifts, particularly those designated by the donor, clearly be encouraged and solicited *as* gifts, to serve the organization's mission and objectives without conflicts of interest.

Again, few authors would surpass Aristotle in his sensitivity to "public standards," properly defined, given his view that the ultimate purpose of philanthropy is to enhance "the public good" by ethical means. In the case of the college donor, we have no reason to suspect an unethical source of wealth—not at least to the degree we may suspect it among those we classically identify with the history of American philanthropy.

THE CLASSIC PHILANTHROPIST

Perhaps it is enough to concede that a segment of modern-day organized philanthropy follows hard on the heels of wealth gained at the expense of human life, destruction of the environment, and harm to the health and well-being of untold numbers of people. No doubt by utilitarian standards the economic impact those great leaders of industry and finance—less charitably called "robber barons"—made on the nation, has been for the public good. However, a cost/benefit analysis of the trade-off is absurd, unless human life and dignity have a purely economic value. Although Aristotle might have commended John D. Rockefeller for his sense of justice in establishing a foundation to compensate for the killing of innocent children at his mine in Colorado, the action could hardly redeem him for the careless conditions that allowed it to happen, nor would his impressive endowment qualify as uncommon beneficence.

Still, while philanthropy as we know it may have been born of questionable lineage, it has long since transcended the means by which its original character was imprinted. Generally, philanthropy today is both honorable and impressive. To his enduring credit Andrew Carnegie led the way with his generous gifts—which he also thoughtfully justified in his classic essay, *The Gospel of Wealth*.[13] In fact, though he may not have intended it so, the essay is Carnegie's way of addressing Aristotle's challenge at the outset of this chapter.

Still, as Aristotle's views imply, if the good these wealthy individuals have done has made up for the bad, that is only fair, a matter of justice, not of philanthropy. The ethics of each of these great virtues deserves its own moral character.

For Aristotle, the wealthy—by definition, persons capable of making unusually large gifts—have a unique responsibility. They are ethically obligated through the use of their wealth to improve society. They may be very successful at what they do, and admired for it; but they have a responsibility that goes beyond their ability as business persons, industrialists, bankers, or professionals to make money.

This responsibility should encourage nonprofit fundraising volunteers and professionals who puzzle about why people give, or what incentive or "hot button" to employ in approaching them. If Aristotle is right, then to realize their potential as human beings the wealthy *ought* to be generous, and be encouraged to be so for their own well-being and that of others.

While the ideal of philanthropy is to be virtuous both in making and distributing one's wealth, Aristotle, like Jesus, held that it is more blessed to give than to receive. True, we admire the person with the Midas touch, but it is not morally admirable in the absence of a disposition to be generous.

To Aristotle, there is an interrelationship: *it is better to perform good actions than to refrain from bad ones*. As we shall see in chapter 2, this is directly contrary to the tendency in American culture today to believe that it's all right to do whatever you want, as long as it's harmless. While this belief may be very seductive as a moral guide, it is a weak substitute for well-grounded freedom of choice and action; and it leaves dangerously open the question of what is harmful, and to whom.

Aristotle's point applies to both the donor (or grantmaker) and the professional fundraiser (and volunteer): the idea is to regularly acquire funds by actively ethical means, and distribute them well. In their giving, donors will seek no favors designed to increase their resources; they should in this respect sharply separate how they give from how they acquire. And in their receiving, as we shall see in the following chapters, professionals and volunteers will have to be both artfully and ethically responsible.

The overriding aim for all—donors, grantmakers, fundraisers, and volunteers—is to maximize the public good by furthering worthy objectives, often those no other sector of society can attend to, or attend to as well. As the opening paraphrase from the *Ethics* suggests, the challenge is to direct charitable gifts to the "right persons," presumably virtuous, competent leaders; in the "right amount," that is, a balance of resources and the uses they can serve; and at the "right time," whenever the need is compelling.

THE STEWARDSHIP TRADITION

For stereotypical philanthropists of the recent past, who like the Carnegies have sought to distribute their wealth with maximum impact on society's needs, Aristotle's notion of beneficence is the ideal norm. The peculiar challenge for some, in the face of allegedly dubious business dealings, is to be as ethical in making or replenishing wealth as they are generous in giving it to improve society. Still, the stereotype is too limited; it excludes the enormous generosity represented by people of relatively modest means—in fact, the category in which most donors and volunteers fall. Without some alternative model we must be content either to restrict philanthropy to extraordinary gifts at some arbitrary level, say $1 million or more, or redefine the term.

One equally familiar and more inclusive model—inspired by Jesus in the Christian era—is the basis for the modern, even secular concept of stewardship. This conception of philanthropy has come to include the giving of one's time and talents—the vast spectrum of volunteerism—along with money as a legitimate expression of generosity.

Pre-dating Jesus but basic to his background is the well-known Hebraic tradition of tithing, giving ten percent of one's money or possessions to godly purpose. In the Old Testament, Abraham (Genesis 14) gives a tithe of his battle spoils; and the faithful (Deuteronomy 14, Leviticus 27) are urged to tithe seed, grain, and the firstborn of their cattle and sheep. It was the right thing to do. The prophet Malachi scolded the people for withholding what was rightfully the Lord's, and noted that God greatly rewards those who tithe. Indeed, the practice of giving a tithe of one's income for religious purposes continues among many to this day, though religious giving as a percentage of income has declined over the last 25 years.[14]

Jesus took this charitable tradition a step farther.[15] According to the New Testament accounts (Matthew 19:16–30; Mark 10:17–31; Luke 18:18–30), when asked by the apparently virtuous and also wealthy young stranger (in Luke, a member of the ruling class) what "good" he must do to "enter the kingdom of God," Jesus first made it clear that only God is truly good. In fact, ultimate well-being is, from a religious perspective, itself a gift; it is divinely conferred, not achieved by ethical action.

Nonetheless, Jesus reminded him, striving to keep the Ten Commandments, a Judeo-Christian code of ethics, is a godly obligation in this life. However, when the stranger said he had always kept the Commandments, Jesus replied that the young man needed to do one more thing: to sell his treasures, distribute the funds to the poor, and join in Jesus' cause. Expecting instead to be told of some new ethical laws or rules he should keep, the virtuous young man found Jesus' norms of uncommon beneficence and total commitment too much to ask. Disappointed, he left, which prompted Jesus' well-known hyperbole: "It will be easier for a camel to pass through the eye of a needle than for a rich man to enter the Kingdom"—definitely not, to borrow from Aristotle, an easy matter. Indeed, as Jesus said, it is possible only with the benevolent, otherworldly assistance of God.

It may be that Jesus intended to underscore the total commitment demanded by the godly life, rather than the ethical responsibilities of wealth. However, the Judeo-Christian tradition of stewardship today is often linked with a second biblical story

(Mark 12:41–44 and Luke 21:1–4), that of the poor "widow's mite"—a gift that apparently satisfies Jesus' standard for beneficence. In this story, Jesus is described as observing people, many of them wealthy, make monetary gifts to the temple treasury. As the wealthy make their larger gifts, a poor widow is seen giving two small coins. Jesus remarks that the widow has done more than the others. With more than enough, the wealthy can afford to make large gifts—relatively easy for them to replenish. The widow, however, with less than enough, gives all she had to live on—certainly not an easy matter.

Thus we have two classic models of philanthropy. Jesus' view is more inclusive and unconditional, if also religiously oriented. Aristotle's is the more exclusive and theoretical, an empirical and rational framework for virtue that is grounded in character development independently of divine assistance.

However, the two have much in common in their use and reflection of enduring, universal principles. Jesus urged obedience to the civil and moral precepts of his day, to the point of setting standards that went well beyond the Ten Commandments. He also added several other normative lessons in his famous "Sermon on the Mount." But, when pressed to reduce the morally upright life to its essentials, Jesus seemed to fix on the principle of love, or ultimate respect of others, guided by a self-love grounded ultimately in a benevolent Creator's enduring love for humankind.

Notwithstanding his radically different perspective, Jesus shares with Aristotle the conviction that philanthropy is not only virtuous and basic to well-being, it is among the highest ethical demands for all. Both Jesus and Aristotle also had their followers while they were alive, and continue to have their adherents after their deaths. However, given the total annual contributions to philanthropic causes in this country, it is doubtful that Aristotle could match Jesus historically for volunteer commitment and generosity. Above all, they share a deep concern for character development, and thus for the motives from which moral actions spring.

We know it is easy to exploit or misdirect the charitable tendencies of people. The case of Jim and Tammy Bakker will come to mind along with other charismatic figures who have misused the funds they so effectively but immorally solicited, ostensibly for divine purposes. Yet, when it comes to charity, as we shall see, theirs is hardly the only moral mischief. Unwarily, as well-meaning donors, for example, we may encourage irresponsible charity by giving millions of dollars annually to well-known nonprofits, often in response to a telephone request, without ever asking how the money will be used. Do we as donors deserve to be morally upset to discover later that the nonprofit's fundraising costs (telemarketing is expensive) or administrative salaries and expense may take a third to a half or more of what is given—at the expense of the worthy programs we are moved to support? As ethically responsible donors, fundraising professionals, and nonprofit organizations there are decisive steps we can take besides simply consulting the local Better Business Bureau or the Charities Division of the state's Attorney General's Office to sound and chart the sometimes murky waters of philanthropy.[16]

THE RESPONSIBLE NONPROFIT

In chapter 2 we will examine in greater detail the modern-day counterparts to the ethics of Aristotle and Jesus. At this point, however, it is important to recognize that moral responsibility is not only a personal matter, defined for the individual agent. It is also an *organizational* matter in which, for many of us, individual and corporate roles intersect. The challenge is how to make this intersection ethically responsible.

A recent case may serve to illustrate the difficulty. A society made up of influential persons was formed ostensibly to raise private funds solely to support a nonprofit foundation created by the state legislature to govern a major community institution. The society played its role very well, and succeeded in raising several hundred thousand dollars. However, instead of turning the funds over to the foundation, the society used them to enhance its own operational budget and promotional efforts; in fact, it worked to replace the foundation. When the foundation challenged the action, the society successfully (legally) fended it off—with money it had originally raised for the foundation—and retained the remaining funds for itself.

We sense there is something wrong here, but where, and why? What is it to be an accountable nonprofit organization?

For grantmaking organizations as well as nonprofits, their professionals and volunteers, the need to play one's role in an ethically responsible manner clearly justifies the efforts to develop and promulgate effective codes of ethics. Many corporations have developed model codes for their employees; and fundraisers are familiar with such efforts by national organizations such as the National Society of Fund Raising Executives, the Association for Healthcare Philanthropy, the American Association of Fund Raising Counsel, the Council for the Advancement and Support of Education, and the National Committee on Planned Giving.

One of the most thoughtful and ambitious attempts to encourage and guide nonprofit organizations, both grantmakers and grantseekers, to develop their own codes of ethics is the report, *Ethics and the Nation's Voluntary and Philanthropic Community: Obedience to the Unenforceable.*[17]

The work takes its lead from the phrase by England's Lord Justice of Appeal, John Fletcher Moulton, and his conviction that ethical individuals and organizations show greatness by their readiness to obey the rules they impose on themselves. This readiness is fundamental to the "public trust," the bond created when individuals freely associate for their common good. In fact, at the philanthropic level, trust is the single most important—and fragile—ethical relationship between donors and nonprofits. Ironically, though Aristotle and other ethicists say little or nothing about it (see chapter 2), beneficence and charity are ethically unthinkable apart from trust.

Written by a distinguished committee under the auspices of Independent Sector, the report provides a three-tiered rationale for setting and practicing high standards of ethical behavior based on the committee's sense of the values essential to society. The committee's list of values, types of ethical responsibility, and applicable examples are uncommonly useful to nonprofit practitioners, and bear repeating here:

Common to all voluntary and philanthropic organizations, according to the committee, there are values that represent a collective good in which ethical responsibility is rooted. They include:

(a) commitment beyond self, basic to civil society; (b) compliance with the law; (c) "obedience to the unenforceable" beyond the law; (d) acknowledgment of the public good and the trust on which it depends; (e) respect for the value and dignity of the individual; (f) appreciation for tolerance, diversity, and social justice; (g) public accountability; (h) openness and honesty; and (i) prudent use of resources.

Briefly, according to the report, we experience the demands for ethical responsibility on three levels: (1) obeying the law; (2) going beyond the law to do what we know to be right, even when tempted otherwise because of the cost; and, (3) wanting to act rightly, but not always knowing how to resolve apparently conflicting ethical values. The committee helpfully provides examples of how the values that organizations share can suffer from the failure to be ethically responsible at each of these levels:

1. For voluntary and philanthropic institutions, obeying the law is a given. As their role implies, according to the committee, trustees have the first responsibility for compliance with the law, but staff and volunteers share in this responsibility according to their separate roles. For example, for an organization to hire without attention to statutes bearing on equal employment opportunity is illegal and contrary to (e) above, respect for the value and dignity of the individual. Again, filing inaccurate or misleading information is not only illegal—misrepresenting the organization disregards (h), the honesty we value.

2. Going beyond the law ("obedience to the unenforceable") is more difficult when often the cost or inconvenience or a member's personal interest is at odds with what the organization knows is right. For a member to file unreasonably high or "padded" travel or conference expenses is unethical in relation to (a), commitment beyond self, and not in the best interests of the organization. It is also a form of lying and thus contrary to (h), the honesty we value. Again, contrary to a more prudent use of the organization's resources, (i) above, it would, according to the report, be unethical for the director, in lieu of salary, to receive a percentage of funds raised by the organization.

3. The most difficult level of ethical responsibility is posed by cases where the choice is not between black and white, right and wrong, but between competing alternatives, both of which seem good. For example, should a corporate foundation that answers to its shareholders fund an outstanding proposal from its most critical detractor organization? Both parties operate from "enlightened self-interest," but between competing values such as (d), the relationship of trust the foundation seeks to further with the public, and (f), the tolerance it requires of its shareholders, the case presents the dilemma of serving one public good only at the expense of another.

As we shall see in the chapters that follow, the resolution and justification of conflicting or competing values goes to the heart of ethical decision-making. Indeed, it distinguishes one ethical framework from another. For its part, however, the committee can only recommend the overall strategies and measures of accountability that may enable philanthropic organizations to become ethically more responsible.

Minimally, the report recommends, every organization should adopt a "credo," a succinct statement of what it hopes to accomplish through its mission; and it should conduct an annual ethics "audit," based on three questions: (1) have legal requirements been met?; (2) are current practices contrary to the organization's credo?; and (3) have changes brought about a need for new ethical choices?

Larger organizations, according to the report, should extend their efforts to develop a supportive set of codes or standards, to involve all of their constituencies in the process, and to infuse the process and the documents into the culture of the total organization. There is no reason, however, why nonprofits of every size would not benefit from the development of a working code of ethics, guided by the process suggested in the final chapter.

Clearly, no overall strategies could present a more appropriate challenge to nonprofit grantmakers, fundraisers, volunteers, and the constituencies they serve today. There are few weaknesses in the committee's work, except perhaps the lack of a clear distinction between responsible role-playing and ethical decision-making. As we learn from Aristotle, the two are not always the same. The task is to blend them appropriately where they intersect, namely in the nonprofit's code of ethics.

The problem with codes, as we shall see, is that they are neither self-clarifying nor self-justifying without an accompanying, ongoing program of ethical self-examination.

To encourage such programs, and to modestly complement the work of the Independent Sector committee, two other strategies remain. One is to devise a model that enables practitioners in nonprofits to develop and regularly test an effective organizational code of ethics. The other strategy is more fundamental and prior to the first. Briefly, it is to describe and exemplify *the elements of a framework for principled action* that will help professional and volunteer practitioners to understand and embody what it means to think and act in an ethically responsible manner. This is our next task.

Two   A Matter of Principle

To argue, as Aristotle does, that philanthropy is a mark of humanity at its best is one thing; to hold it as a moral responsibility equal with justice is quite another. Not only is beneficence an admirable trait; it is a virtuous lifestyle that those with the capacity for it *ought* to develop.

While others, notably Jesus, also held generosity to be high among human virtues, no one presents its value as persuasively as Aristotle. He is virtually unique among classical philosophers for his attempt to describe the ideal philanthropist.

However, the problem for most of us is not the ideal, but the practical. The practical problem, as the well-known metaphor suggests, is knowing in each morally demanding situation of life where to draw the lines. Although Aristotle formulates the ethical standard for virtuous behavior and a general formula of moderation for making decisions of a morally related sort, his principles do little to help us decide precisely which action will be neither too much nor too little.

Many other great thinkers have also devised frameworks for ethical decision-making. While this is not the place to review them all, it is helpful to know something about the most enduring, particularly the two or three that are applicable to ethical philanthropy. Before that, however, we should also review some elementary but essential requirements for thinking and acting in an ethically responsible way. Based on both classroom and practical experience, these elements are basic for helping practitioners develop their own framework for deciding right actions.[1]

THE ART OF KNOWING RIGHT FROM WRONG

Ethics, or morality—the terms are often used interchangeably—is the art of choosing and doing what is right, just, or good. As we noted, Aristotle's middle ground between extremes assumes a fundamental and generally acceptable conviction: there are limits beyond which it is imprudent or counterproductive, if not self-destructive, for human beings to go. This conviction is at least intuitively true for most. The middle, moral ground is the simplest basis for distinguishing the good or the right from their immoral extremes.

To act responsibly within acknowledged limits is about all Aristotle can offer as a universal and practical moral framework. As a student of geometry and physics, he is well aware that moral decision-making lacks their deductive rigor; it yields only what is for the most part true. It cannot offer certainty because, unlike the constants that characterize geometry, ethics deals with a notoriously unpredictable variable: the human individual.

Thus, determining what is good and doing the right thing amid a plethora of individual circumstances is more an art than a science. While Aristotle's principle of the mean between extremes is widely, perhaps universally acknowledged, one's particular moral choice is relative in an all too familiar way: it all depends on the person and the circumstances. The right, the good, and the just may well turn out to be the mean between extremes, but the middle way for me may not be the same for everyone—or even anyone—else. It's relative.

The relativism of Aristotle's principle can also characterize organizational behavior. For example: Is it right for a nonprofit that specializes in counseling and temporary shelter for persons subject to various abuses and addictions to support itself with regular contributions from the local gambling casino? It all depends, we say, on how effective the nonprofit is, who benefits from the counseling, how dependent the nonprofit is on the funds, how beneficial the gambling profits are for the welfare of the minorities who own the casinos, etc. Since doing the right thing is relative to a number (who knows how many) of particular circumstances, the main thing is to avoid the extremes of decision-making by satisfying all the conditions—including competing or conflicting interests.

Unfortunately, where ethical principles are vague or lack common applicability, we can (rather artfully) cook up conditions that tend to dissipate apparent moral tensions. An adequate ethical framework demands a surer, more discerning kind of art, for which we need clear and compelling principles. Being artful to achieve goodness and justice may be the single greatest challenge to beings whose ultimate goal in life is well-being, or happiness. How does this artfulness emerge? And why should it ever go beyond pure self-interest (egoism) to the interests of others (altruism)?

MORAL PROMPTINGS

English philosophers such as Shaftesbury (1671–1713) and Hutcheson (1694–1746) held that human nature is imbued with "moral sense"—benevolent passions that dispose us to virtue and public interest.[2] Guided by reason, they suggested, we are moved to regard "the greatest happiness for the greatest number"—a formula subsequently borrowed by the Utilitarians, as we shall see—as an important criterion of the goodness of an action.

The ancient conviction that there are limits is basic to another kind of moral sense, the modern-day notion of *conscience*, where most of us with moral sensitivities begin. "Having scruples" comes to mind: we are shocked by what we regard as shameful (unscrupulous) behavior, and surprised that a person's morally questionable act reflects no apparent doubt or hesitation, despite a widely accepted behavior to the contrary. Some say conscience is innate, a divinely implanted alarm that goes off whenever we go beyond the limits established by religious convictions. Others say it is a learned response to limits we have been taught to honor in an environment of law, rules, cultural mores, or family influences.

Whatever its source, conscience is readily acknowledged as a kind of moral prompting, and an important reminder that for most of us morality does not begin in a vacuum. Most of us are equipped early on with a rough and ready sense, not always adequate, of how we "ought" and "ought not" to behave. Clearly, among some—the perpetrators of senseless acts of abuse or violence that strike us as "unconscionable"—the prompting of conscience is a mere whimper in the presence of more intimidating inner forces such as greed, revenge, domination, fear, or hunger.

When asked how always being hungry affected her outlook on life, a poor but devoutly Hindu woman from India replied, "It makes it hard to think about God." Indeed, such tensions characterize the moral struggle.

Conscience aside, the first problem many people have is to know when they are dealing with a moral matter, not a non-moral concern that falls outside the bounds of moral consideration. Beyond the practical confusion, the problem is profound. Watergate, for example, has come to represent a classic kind of moral naivete in which the agents of deceit, among "the best and the brightest" in government service, pathetically lacked the awareness they had done anything wrong.

The word "ought," because it seems to compel us, is often but not always a clue that we are dealing with a moral matter. To declare that "if you want a good hamburger you ought to go to McDonald's," or, "if you want good rock 'n' roll, (you should) listen to Elvis Presley," does not seem very compelling morally. The claim may identify experiences we value, and value is often associated with morality. However, not everything valuable is moral, and terms like "ought," and its relative "should," serve a larger function in our language than to flag a moral issue.

Again, laws and rules suggest the right thing to do and are an easy step from the moral language of lines and limits. "Playing by the rules," provided we do not make them up as we go along, is another of those meaningful metaphors that goes well beyond game behavior. We devise all kinds of laws, enforce them to achieve order and protection, and presume they are good for our organizations, communities, and society at large. We are taught to uphold the law and never regard ourselves "above" it. Obeying the law, we say, is the right thing to do.

However, law and morality should not be confused. Human concerns for what is right and just go well beyond the various bodies of law. The saying, "one cannot legislate morality," presumes that law is no guarantee of good behavior. Moreover, experience frequently demonstrates the injustices or inadequacies of laws and rules, and the need to rethink them in the light of the moral complexities of life.

That law and morality are different in character is also evident from the continuing debates over fundamental human convictions, for example abortion issues or acts of civil disobedience, in the face of laws we may feel are wrong or unfair. The intent or spirit of legislation may be to achieve justice, but the question whether any given law achieves this purpose is always open to question. Finally, morality, unlike law, is, as Lord Moulton noted, a matter of obeying the unenforceable; laws are enforceable.

Aristotle narrowed the field of ethics to matters of justice and beneficence. Courage is a virtue, but not a moral responsibility. However, if morality is defined, as it often is, as customary, acceptable—even encouraged—behavior rooted in our culture, then the bounds that distinguish virtue from morality become vague. Moreover, grounding or justifying behavior in mores or customs[3] makes it impossible to hold that moral principles are the same for all. Numerous and profound cultural differences make acceptable or permissible behavior completely relative to a particular time and place.

The view that cultural differences and changing attitudes define morality—"moral relativism"—is a popular and powerful assumption. It suggests that moral absolutes are presumptuous if not absurd. As this way of thinking goes, the real question is how much a particular society will tolerate or condone, and where one personally prefers to draw the line. Apart from enforceable laws and deeply-cherished practices, there are no universally acknowledged moral norms.

As noted in *Habits of the Heart*, an impressive study of American culture a few years ago, we still value the self-reliance and especially the freedom our Founding Fathers believed in. But in a changing world, such values have come to mean independence from "old-fashioned" moral standards. According to the study, we Americans want to develop our own personal belief systems, to be liberated from the archaic religious and institutional duties our parents knew and accepted. We want to define our individual selves by the values (read: idiosyncratic preferences) *we* choose, and be governed by *results* to know whether our actions prove useful or consistent. In short, we are utilitarians. For us, there are no objectifiable criteria for right, wrong, good, or evil; only the self and its feelings are moral guides. Rigid moral standards inhibit progress; nothing is absolute save death, so we must be adaptable, "go with the flow." Thus, the authors of the study conclude, the popular American lifestyle is a radically "unencumbered and improvisational self."[4]

In a permissive, individualistic, and freedom-loving culture such as ours, this belief encourages the attitude that every moral opinion is of equal value—that morality is a very personal, private matter, and (rightfully) should not and (logically) cannot be questioned. To acknowledge this attitude as a "right," a very ambiguous term, is said to presuppose the most fundamental of moral concerns: individual respect.

While outwardly very attractive, the attitude is impractical and self-defeating. Morality may not require absolutes—with the possible exception of respect for individual rights!—but it does require some generally acceptable basis for resolving conflicting values, the tensions characteristic of ethics.

For example, a common form of the concern for respect, too easily proposed, is the venerable Golden Rule: "Do unto others as you would have them do unto you." Charitably speaking, this popular norm seems to rest on the conviction that if every person would be more considerate, sensitive, and respectful of others, the world would be a better place. Ironically, the Rule can also be intended simply to shield one's personal interests against responsible demands by others that one does not happen to like.

The problem with the Rule as a general norm is that it cannot stand by itself without careful qualification. For example, it can also be understood to assume that anything that is in one's own self-interest is also in the self-interest of others, presumably a good thing. But surely that goes too far. Suppose as an officer of a nonprofit I decide that padding my expenses "repays" me for the inconvenience of travel: Should I condone or encourage the same behavior in others on the staff?

If understood to support what is in everyone's "best" interests, the Rule would perhaps be more acceptable. However, that can leave open the question of what is in one's best interests. Generally, the Rule works best when it presupposes the action of a rational, psychologically normal agent; one who always attempts to do what is right or good for every person, guided by a proper sense of self-respect. Aside from the widespread religious understanding of the Rule, the most influential philosophical use of it is, as we shall see later, commonly associated with the eighteenth-century German philosopher Immanuel Kant (1724–1804).

CONFLICT AND CHOICE

Ethics is sometimes defined as the conflict of values, where "values" are distinguished from observable "facts." The distinction derives from writings of the Scottish philosopher David Hume (1711–1776), who observed that debates about what "ought to be" are really about differences of personal preferences, subjective convictions or individual values. They are not to be confused with claims for what "is," that is, facts or matters of existence whose truth depends on what is objectively, empirically the case. Hume also argues for the existence of an innate "moral sense" in humanity. However, by equating moral judgments with personal preferences, he is probably responsible for influencing a rather sophisticated, current-day form of moral relativism.[5]

Hume's enduring insight—that one cannot logically derive (moral) values from (empirical) facts—is particularly telling against behaviorists, trends analysts, pollsters, and countless well-meaning people who have been tempted to argue from the way things are, to the way they ought to be. Clearly, from the fact that "everybody is doing it," it does not follow that it is right or ought to be done.

Like "ought," the term "value" can also be vaguely and ambiguously used. Opinions about what is good or right, behavioral dispositions, emotional needs, preferences, inclinations, desires, religious convictions, and political beliefs all qualify as personal values, and thus vary greatly among us. Our values tend to reflect individual self-interest, or what we may believe is "good" for us, and it is hard to avoid the feeling that, respect for others aside, one's own values are better or more appropriate than those of others.

Thus, selecting a suitable framework for moral decision-making poses a critical choice for every thoughtful person: between (a) conceding that since every value is of equal merit, one should aim at situational expediency or compromise; and (b) finding less relative, more timeless, immutable norms for consistently evaluating conflicting or competing moral claims.

In an extreme form, (a) is a strategy embodied by Machiavelli (1469–1527) in his classic work *The Prince*, where the end—for the Prince, power, authority—justifies whatever means at any time are necessary to achieve and secure it.[6] In a more benign form it is the kind of agreement sought, for example, by disputing representatives of management and labor, or by legislators that support partisan differences or the special, sometimes competing interests of their constituents.

The challenge of (b), to find more enduring standards by which differing values are judged, is a more difficult task for ethics. Since some moral issues present a quandary or dilemma for us, opposing values at times not only seem to carry the same weight, but may also present radically exclusive alternatives. Søren Kierkegaard (1813–1855), the nineteenth-century Danish thinker, termed this an "either/or," a paradox of alternatives that existentially leaves no room for compromise.

The classic case he poses, in *Fear and Trembling*, is that of the Old Testament figure Abraham who is instructed by God to sacrifice his only son, Isaac, in direct contradiction to God's own commandment against killing. By every human and divine standard, Abraham knows it is wrong to murder, knows it is irrational to go through with God's shocking demand. Yet, in the face of this "absurdity"—a key criterion also for Kant, as we shall see—he prepares to do it. Grounded solely by his faith that it is the right thing to do, he trusts that God will restore everything—which, as the story goes, does happen. To Kierkegaard there are crucial situations in life that demand a "higher," non-compromising, all-encompassing principle for deciding what is right. Faith in God is that principle.[7]

While most ethical dilemmas nonprofit practitioners face are not this extreme, they are no less difficult to resolve without some higher, governing principle, however inadequate. For example, ethicist Daniel Callahan states one of the most pervasive if implicit principles for moral decision-making today in this way: "One may act in any way one chooses so far as one does not do harm to others." Callahan dubs it "the minimalist ethic."[8] Of course, what constitutes "harm" is itself problematic, and a prime candidate for moral relativism. However, the formula—which presupposes the unqualified principle of respect for others—does seem to offer a "higher" standard for resolving conflicts among competing values.

While, as Callahan seems to argue, this minimalist principle may be totally inadequate for the times in which we live, it helps make the point that what is ethically appropriate first emerges from the conflict of values as a higher-level "ought" or obligation, arising out of the need to make a moral decision.

In fact, it is useful to distinguish the "moral relativism" based on cultural differences from the domain of "ethics." Ethics, we can say, is concerned to find principles on which all can rely, in every generation, to justify what ought to be done. On the relative-to-absolute spectrum, ethics is the desire to get as close as possible to the absolute. Unlike morality that is culturally determined, ethical decision-making is the practice of justifying through reason and experience what is good and right on the basis of generally if not universally acceptable and enduring principles.

SELF-EXAMINATION

Conflict, especially over ethical matters, is often due in part to lack of communication and understanding. Patiently clarifying the source of the tension is essential and may go a long way toward resolving it. It is helpful to approach an ostensibly ethical issue with the following considerations in mind:

1. *Clarify facts and terms.* Revealing the tensions, the key issues, is the task. Clarify the facts of the case, and especially terms like "value," "good," and "right" that are often vaguely and/or ambiguously used. For example, to say that something is valuable is a *vague* claim; it leaves open the questions: how valuable, in what respect, and to whom? It is rela-

tive, a matter of degree; something may be more or less valuable than some other known value, etc. A term such as "right" can be ambiguous, having two or more meanings, for example: a right one has by birth, a right conferred by the Constitution, a right agreed upon by contract, etc.

2. *Examine assumptions.* For example, if I say you should never harm another, I assume you have the ability to do so. Immanuel Kant, the ethicist we will consider later, made the assumption explicit in the formula: " 'ought' implies 'can.' " The formula clarifies the belief (also held by Aristotle) that to be held ethically responsible, that is, praiseworthy or blameworthy, you must have the capacity to act. Again, "Always tell the truth" assumes that you know what the truth is.

3. *Define key concepts and abstract ideas.* Actually, to convey our ideas we define them in many different ways, using, for example: (a) observed or assumed experience of reality ("Hail is frozen rain"); (b) concepts or processes unique to science, mathematics, or technology ("A byte is the smallest unit of computer data space"); (c) colloquial or conventional expressions ("That's cool!"); and (d) meanings we stipulate to establish a common point of departure for discussion ("By 'conservative' I mean . . . "). Until the truth of what we *mean* is established, no one kind of definition is most accurate or "real." The first thing is to understand how we are using the ideas or concepts under discussion; only then can we evaluate the grounds that will make their definition adequate or inadequate.

4. *Be objective, genuinely curious.* Socrates was regarded the wisest of the ancients for insisting he was really ignorant about ideas like goodness and justice—ideas that others discussed with seeming ease but, upon further examination, with less understanding than he. His approach was to accept what others believed as true, unless in the course of questioning them he found their beliefs based on inconsistencies or questionable assumptions. His purpose was to be as objective and dispassionate as possible, to distinguish reasonable belief from mere opinion.

5. *Try to be reasonable.* In the broadest sense this means to be open, educable, prepared to make up your mind when the evidence seems to warrant it. In a narrower, logical sense it means that one's beliefs conform with rules for being rational. For example, one cannot (rationally) claim both that something is the case and that it is not the case at the same time in the same respect. Intuitively, a mark of rationality is the apparent capacity normal persons have for sensing when a conclusion compellingly "follows," and when it does not "follow" from the judgments (premises) that precede it. While most of us pay lip service to the need for rationality, few of us consistently apply it. Generally, the capacity and readiness to acknowledge *consistency* or *inconsistency* in one's expression and behavior—which we all regularly insist on—is basic to what it means to be a rational human being.

SELF-WORTH

The notion of individual respect, noted above, implies a fundamental conviction about human worth. An ethical framework presupposes such convictions, often both scientific and metaphysical, about the nature and destiny of humankind.

For example, why *should* we be ethical? The question is tricky, logically circular, presupposing an ethical response. For Aristotle, the belief that there are prudent limits to human action is one reason to draw the right lines. Another is that drawing them rightly serves to realize one's potential. Why, to what end? To experience well-being, happiness, the ultimate goal. Why? To Aristotle it makes no sense to press the question further: It is not problematic; it is self-evident, like the "truths" we hold in the Declaration of Independence.

Many ethicists of the past have developed theories of self-worth on which to ground their views. Immanuel Kant, for example, was impressed by the notion that human nature is endowed with two "selves" that regularly "converse," argue, explore feelings and ideas with each other. The one self is disposed by impulse, passion, and inclination; the other is independent and capable of reason, right thinking. Like the French thinker Jean-Jacques Rousseau (1712–1778), he believed in a "good will" common to all, in which all interests coincide and are truly "free," if only people would be guided by their capacity to be reasonable, not emotional. Appealing to reason brings out one's "better self," a self one can truly respect and love. That is the self we also respect in others, and the self we want others to respect in us. In fact, self-worth of this sort was so important to Kant that he made it a cardinal rule of his ethics to treat every person always as an end, never a means to an end.

The ultimate questions about the meaning of life, such as whether goodness and justice are matters of self-realization (Aristotle), or are attainable only with divine assistance (Kierkegaard), in this world or another, are unavoidable, and the answers we devise ultimately rest on conviction. These convictions go to the heart of the human condition with which ethical action is concerned. They are the ultimate lines we can draw, the final ground or justification we can provide for the ethical stance we take—so ultimate, as the word implies, they are like Euclid's axioms, needing no grounds of their own.

The grounds for ethically justifying our day-to-day actions take various forms, but traditionally three are predominant:

1.   For example, to John Stuart Mill (1806–1873), the nineteenth-century English philosopher of Utilitarianism—still one of the most powerful ethical frameworks, as we shall see below—the general weight of human experience, or *empirical evidence*, is most persuasive.

2.   To Kant, who represents another of the most important frameworks, *rational intuition*, or the capacity to be consistent, reasonable, is most conducive to human self-worth, and most reliable.

3.   Kierkegaard, representing a religious view, to a point agrees with Kant: the best ethical framework would rely mainly on principles grounded in reason. Yet, sadly he argues in *Fear and Trembling*, no ethical framework based on reason alone can resolve the existential quandaries of personal experience exemplified in the godly—and to reason, absurd—de-

mand to Abraham to sacrifice his son, Isaac. To Kant the action is absurd, it is murder, and murder is unconditionally wrong. To Kierkegaard, only the power of faith—humanly speaking, a kind of *passion*—or divine intervention is the final hope for justification.

Indeed, throughout the history of ethics philosophers have argued whether reason, experience, or passion ultimately rules, or should rule, human action.

Whatever the grounds, the end we seek is a profile of the morally-directed *worth* or value we place on ourselves and others. We tend to define this worth in terms of fundamental convictions that, like a personal Bill of Rights, may include freedom, equality, sanctity of life, privacy, justice, and respect for human (even animal) rights of various kinds. To many ethicists, such as Kant, self-love or self-respect, appropriately qualified to describe the human condition at its best is basic to the respect we owe to others. Such convictions also reveal just how self- or other-directed our ethical framework is, that is, how egoistic or altruistic we are.[9]

THE CENTRALITY OF TRUST

A related concept, actually a concomitant expectation of the principle of respect for others, is *trustworthiness*.[10] As noted in chapter 1, to be worthy of trust is perhaps the most cherished aim underlying the values common to all philanthropic organizations. It is a remarkable fact that ethicists as influential throughout history as Aristotle, Kant, and Mill—with the possible exception of Kierkegaard—provide no place (except, perhaps, implicitly) among their key virtues, values, and principles for the idea of trust. We can probably thank John Locke (1632–1704), the English philosopher who inspired the language of the Declaration of Independence, for arguing that government is a "public trust," and thus for instilling in American society the concept of trusteeship.

Thinkers may have omitted the idea of trust because it is so fundamental as to be assumed or unspoken. Principles such as promise-keeping, truth-telling, and justifiable rights are logically related to, if not dependent on, trust. For nonprofit fundraisers, volunteers, and foundation staff it is hard to imagine beneficence without trust. Without this "good will toward mankind," in the ancient sense, philanthropy would never materialize.

Trust differs from conventional principles by being conspicuously relational. From the outset, trust is the relationship that enables one person to associate willingly, voluntarily with others, prior to any purpose they might devise for their common good. As such, trust is dynamic. It develops, grows, as promises are kept, obligations honored, words embodied that consistently demonstrate character worthy of confidence. It also shrinks and vanishes, sometimes beyond recall, as actions belie the claim that a trustworthy relationship exists.

Philanthropic organizations thrive only as they sustain public trust. Foundations, themselves trustees of the funds they distribute, make grants to those they trust to use the funds prudently, honestly, and effectively. Private donors give—and will continue to give—to organizations that steward their contributions in accordance with the cause. Like bank trust departments, planned giving programs are regularly entrusted with the lifetime assets of the charitably inclined. And nonprofit trustees, volunteers who often also contribute a portion of their own personal assets, are entrusted with the fiduciary well-being of the organization. Indeed, if there were no other reason to be ethical in philanthropic work, trustworthiness would be sufficient.

ACTING ON PRINCIPLE

Because we can make the right judgment but fail to act on it, a framework for thinking and acting in an ethical way employs principles or rules both to justify moral judgment and to guide action. The Apostle Paul made the difference into a fundamental caveat for Christian ethics, to support the need for divine assistance: "The good that we would, we cannot; and the good that we can, we will not".[11] That is, neither good intention nor action is sufficient to bring about goodness or well-being. Divine power alone, through the only truly good and benevolent will of God, is ethically efficacious.

From a secular point of view the major presumption in the use of principles or rules is that they are widely if not universally effective. They endure through time, space, and cultural change. They can serve as reliable standards by which to develop character or inform right-making action.

To adhere to such durable standards is apparently important to us, considering how frequently we insist that following a certain course of action is "a matter of principle" for us. In fact, we all seem to share this unwritten rule for thinking and acting ethically: whatever one's ethical convictions, they must be acted on with consistency (logically), and avoid any hypocrisy that reflects the attitude, "Do as I say, not as I do."

ETHICAL ADEQUACY

An ethical judgment typically makes a claim that a particular action is good or bad. The judgment seems to impose an obligation on the one responsible for the action to continue or correct it. Unlike law, the force of the obligation is based on a mutual conviction of what is right and wrong, just and good. Thus, if the judgment is justified or ethically adequate, it remains for the person at whom it is aimed to do it. It is self-enforced.

The process for justifying an ethical judgment might take the following form:

(c)   *The ethical judgment:* "You went back on your word; that's wrong." Suppose this is challenged: "So what? Why is that wrong?"

(b)   *The ethical principle:* "Because you made a promise, and keeping a promise is a pledge of personal integrity, a basis for mutual agreement and action." That is, the judgment is an instance, in this case a violation, of a general ethical rule or principle. But suppose this rule also is challenged: "So I broke a promise. What's the big deal? Why should I keep my promises?"

(a)   *The governing framework:* "Promise-keeping is generally in the best interests of all, as experience with contracts, agreements, and human relations shows." Or: "Consistent with reason, it is every person's duty." Or: "It is the will of God."

Or: "It is a virtue essential to character and well-being." In short, there is no higher principle to which one can appeal to support one's judgment.

Thus, one's judgment (c) is ethically adequate if justified by rules of inference on the basis of general principle (b) and, if necessary, (a), one's ultimate ground.

Ethical debate in day-to-day experience can be very complex. Although this argument model is spare if not simplistic, it does provide one fundamental guideline: an adequate ethical decision may be derived from a logically related principle or rule to which others can reasonably subscribe.

The final choice of an ethical framework follows from considerations such as the above, and provides the capacity to make ethically adequate decisions. What distinguishes this capacity for practitioners in philanthropy, we shall see, is not so much a framework unique to the profession as it is the range of issues encountered in the line of duty. Matters of trustworthiness, respect for others, truthfulness, public good, private rights—and the ethical principles that serve to justify them—are common to all our relationships. The subject matter, the tensions that characterize it, and our priorities, vary with the situations.

TWO KINDS OF ETHICAL DECISION-MAKING

The existential promptings of Kierkegaard notwithstanding, two kinds of frameworks for ethical decision-making prevail today: *utilitarian*, inspired in various forms by John Stuart Mill; and *formalist* or *deontological* (relating to duty), derived from the monumental writings of Immanuel Kant. Variants of these frameworks are further distinguished as *consequentialism*, denoting emphasis on the interests, effects or ends that would justify an action; and *nonconsequentialism*, holding that inherent duties or rights justify an action. While both classical representatives hold that the rightness of an action depends on its accord with a governing rule or principle, Mill holds that the consequences are everything; Kant holds that doing one's duty irrespective of consequences is paramount.

As we have seen, these two frameworks by no means exhaust

the classic ways we have of thinking about ethical matters. Indeed, ethicist Kenneth Goodpaster probably provides the most satisfactory overview with four major "outlooks": (1) *interest-based*, including self-interested egoism and utilitarianism; (2) *rights-based*, including contractarians who seek the fair distribution of opportunity and wealth in society, and libertarians who appeal to basic freedoms; (3) *duty-based*, which derives its inspiration from Kant, but can be somewhat less individualistic, more devoted to organizational or community responsibilities; and (4) *virtue-based*, after Aristotle and others, with a focus on character development.[12]

We have already given substantial attention to virtue-based ethics (4) in chapter 1. However, by focusing mainly on the outlooks inspired by Mill and Kant in what follows, the aim is to provide practitioners in philanthropy with a fundamental feel for the two ways of thinking and acting they are most likely to encounter. As noted further in chapter 4, Goodpaster's classification also provides the practitioner with an excellent means for analyzing the ethical character of situations he or she will experience.

While Mill's way of thinking is somewhat easier to understand than Kant's, both are very thoughtful and sophisticated theories, and neither can be covered adequately in what follows. They are giants in the history of thought, in fields that range from ethics and theory of knowledge to political affairs; and they deserve much greater attention than they will receive here. For our purposes, however, they serve mainly as classic examples of the major ethical movements they have influenced; alternative frameworks which one might choose to develop and employ in ethical decision-making.

For Mill, the happiness or well-being we all seek is, in his view of human nature, a matter of maximizing pleasure and minimizing pain.[13] Experienced in various ways, this goal is basic to all motivation. However, general experience also demonstrates that by following certain rules, such as keeping promises and telling the truth, we are happiest. As a whole this is what it means to pursue the good life and to be ethical in pursuing it.

Thus, the general principle of what he and others called utilitarianism is: *Any action that on balance is an effective means to a satisfying end, generally "the greatest good for the greatest number," is ethically appropriate.*

In this respect the end or result, if more beneficial than harmful, justifies the means. To calculate "the greatest good," every person is to count as one, and no person for more than one.

The utilitarian framework is powerful, simple to understand and apply. Any course of action consistent with the framework— including certain well-known moral rules grounded in widespread human experience such as truth-telling, equality, promise-keeping, and justice—is justified, or demonstrates its "utility," by its tendency to produce the greatest happiness or goodness for the greatest number of people.

For Kant, who seems to have anticipated and opposed utilitarian thinking, one cannot define "goodness" by reference to personal inclinations and interests, or to outcomes that happen to meet with the satisfaction of most people.[14] They are not, as noted earlier, representative of the human self at its best, nor sufficiently similar or predictable as a whole to serve as a comprehensive norm.

In fact, Kant insists, if anything deserves to be called "good," it is a *good will*, that is, the will to do right and avoid wrong. Acting with good intentions irrespective of consequences or personal feelings is the best way for making an action morally worthy. However, good intentions are not enough. The will is not by nature good, and thus needs guidance in what it ought to do— whether it does it or not—in the form of duties as determined by persons who are truly reasonable.

To Kant, what is most characteristic of ethical action is to *understand one's duty and do it*. That I may be inclined to do the right thing, or produce a beneficial result by my action, is fine—provided above all it is done for the sake of duty. But even when it goes contrary to desire or a good result, duty—a well-intended course of action or maxim, guided by one's rational self or "practical reason"—is what really matters.

Thus, contrary to Mill's greatest happiness principle, Kant's primary rule of ethical action is not an empirical generalization or rule based on what tends to have a good result, or satisfies the interests or inclinations of most people. Rather, to be morally worthy we must do our duty for its own sake, truly free of every other motivation, even the very strong feelings of sympathy and self-love (though they do help to motivate us) we often experience.

What is my duty, my obligation, my ethical responsibility? Guided above all by my rational self, each of my duties must be, in effect, a universal moral law, right for everyone; a law that takes the logical form—hence the label "formalism"—of what Kant calls the "Categorical Imperative": *Act always in such a way that what you intend can at the same time reasonably be expected to apply to every person without exception.*

Initially, we determine our duty in a given situation by attending to our inclinations. But then we have to ask ourselves whether we can at the same time reasonably will our action to be compatible with a universal moral law that follows the form of the Categorical Imperative. For example, suppose I am inclined to deceive a prospective donor about plans my nonprofit has in order to please the prospect and move her or him to make a gift. My inclination takes the form: "Always deceive a prospect about plans for my organization if that would move the prospect to make a contribution." Or, more generally, "Always deceive others when it serves one's purposes to do so." But this maxim or intention is contrary to my ethical duty. I cannot imagine that deceiving others to suit my purposes should become a universal moral law.

Two of Kant's own examples may also be helpful. (1) Suppose I plan to get money by borrowing, promising to pay it back but having no intention to do so. The principle implicit in my action is: "Make false promises when it is expedient to do so." But this is absurd as an instance of the universal, Categorical Imperative; if promises can be broken that easily, no one would rely on them. (2) A person is in great need, whom I can help; but I prefer not to do so. My decision takes the form: "You need never help someone in great need if you don't feel like it." Though there is nothing rationally self-contradictory about making this maxim a moral imperative, nevertheless I should not will it, according to Kant, knowing that some day I may be in need myself. (This example has an obvious application to charity.)

Thus, reminiscent of the Golden Rule, but superior to the unqualified version in chapter 1, Kant's imperative assures us that what you "do unto others" is grounded not in personal or group self-interest, but in duty embedded in a transcendent concept of self-respect that rationally compels respect for others. All the rules that tend to justify one's ethical actions, such as promise-keeping or equal and just treatment of others, are implied by this fundamental imperative. While Kant does seem to allow us to be "prudent" at times when it prevents us from doing things that might disrupt the general stability of life, that too should be done for the sake of duty.

Kant is also important for treating the concept of individual rights as a concomitant of duties (see Goodpaster, above). The idea of rights which I may have by nature or by virtue of authority is a major theme in the history of thought, and the current concern for human rights is no less compelling. For Kant, while not every duty may have a corresponding right, the "perfect" obligation for me is one that gives another the right to expect it. For example, if it is my duty not to harm you, then you have a right to expect no intentional harm from me.

Today, we are uncommonly preoccupied and often confused about the claims of individual and corporate rights throughout American society. Many kinds and qualities of rights are claimed. For example, by vesting government as a public trust (Locke), we have the right in America to expect a concern for our general welfare, and the right to alter government if it fails in its purpose. As an individual I may also claim rights that are both negative (freedom from interference) and positive (welfare assistance); both general (the right not to be murdered) and specific (the right to be compensated for work).[15] To justify my rights I may appeal to those guaranteed by the government, or to those I feel I have by nature, such as threats to my dignity or worth as a human being. The point is that a claim to a right requires qualification and, above all, justification.

In America and elsewhere, the imperativist outlook is difficult to hold. The appeal of utilitarian thinking in ethical and other matters is powerful and pervasive. For example, it is fundamental in strategic organizational planning, with its emphasis on measurable results and a favorable ratio of benefits to costs (harm); in applied science, which seeks to replicate the useful findings of research, to improve health, the environment, living conditions, etc.; in legislation which is designed and enacted to achieve a greater public good; and in program after program throughout the nonprofit sector aimed at bringing about social betterment.

Without a doubt this way of thinking particularly for science and business is indispensable and of great value to society. What the Kantian outlook challenges is the *ethical* efficacy of "goodness" defined by consequences that most satisfy most people, independently of a more objective, universally applicable, and ideally rational moral order.

Both ethical frameworks have their weaknesses. A major inconsistency in utilitarian or consequentialist thinking is its implicit reliance on non-utilitarian principles. Evaluative principles, intuitively or rationally derived, are needed to restrict the wide range of possible alternative courses of action, from which the one providing the "greatest good" is chosen; or to rank-order the qualitatively different values of "happiness" that can define what is good and beneficial, evil and harmful; or to determine whose perspective is best to weigh the harms and benefits; or to decide precisely which of an action's consequences, and when, is an appropriate test of its goodness.[16]

The Kantian or imperativist position suffers initially by presuming that what I know to be right and reasonable is compelling enough to overcome any contrary inclination or self-interest I might have. It is true by definition that a reasonable person is logically consistent, but—with the possible exception of Spock in "Star Trek"—that is a very high standard for most of us. As the saying goes, "the road to hell is paved with good intentions." Still, Kant could agree. He is a rigorist whose chief interest is to define the rational conditions under which a course of action would qualify as truly moral, not merely as satisfying or expedient. But perhaps, as Kierkegaard suggests, that is expecting too much of human action and reason.

Of greater concern for non-consequentialists like Kant is the practical resolution of sometimes conflicting principles, such as truth-telling and the sanctity of human life. The conflict arises, for example, when a hostage of terrorists is told that by refusing to videotape his captors' false claims, a fellow hostage may be tortured or killed. Clearly, it is troubling to hold that truth-telling is prior to possible torture or death in this or any situation. However, lying to avoid the latter would then seem to depend on some higher principle, perhaps the sanctity of life, which in turn entails a hierarchy among such principles. This hierarchy is also suggested in Kant's own example (2) above, where the rule to help another in distress seems to value the welfare of others before one's own.

In response, Kant might sidestep the apparent dilemma by holding that lying may seem like the *prudent* thing to do in this case, but it is never truly *moral* unless done for the sake of duty. In fact, one might rescue Kant by viewing the entire conflict of principles, both of which are universally obligatory, as one instance of the Categorical Imperative, reflecting a single principle. For example: "It is always prudent to lie, if lying will save another's life." However, the general spirit of Kant's writings provides little evidence for treating conflicts in this way. For Kant, one's duty is paramount: lying is wrong, even if prudent; telling the truth is right, regardless of its life-threatening consequences.

Another concern for classical utilitarians is the priority of the majority or greatest number over that of the individual. It is a question of self-worth, or ultimate love of self. For Kant, the individual agent (and every individual) is supreme, regarded always as an end (an alternate form of the Categorical Imperative), never a means to be exploited either by another or by the majority. If individual sacrifice is ethically appropriate in a particular case for one—a case in which one cannot (rationally) imagine an exception—it is imperative for all. Though it is not common throughout the world, in America we show uncommon attention to claims of individual rights, such as sanctity of life, freedom, dignity, and privacy for all.

SUMMING UP

To think and act ethically a practitioner typically has a choice of two major frameworks, with many variations: consequentialism (utilitarianism) and non-consequentialism (formalism); the greatest probable good versus the most rational universal duty.[17] We can always try to do the right thing for constituents and colleagues by calculating the probability of benefits over harm that will result from our intended action; or, we can attempt to do what would with the best of intentions consistently apply to every person regardless of the consequences. It's a choice between governing principles.

In either case it is "a matter of principle" and thus undergirds what by experience or reason we have come to regard as a common core of normative guidelines such as truth-telling, justice, promise-keeping, equality, and the like. However, as Aristotle would say, to be right more often than wrong takes artfulness as well as consistency.

Like Aristotle, my approach is that being ethical is more artful than scientific. There are recognized principles of vital ethical importance to human life, but they necessarily leave room for interpretation and options. Ethics is a matter of using sound judgment about what is right, guided by enduring principles that, unlike mathematics, offer no certainty—barring divine intervention—that our intended action is always appropriate.

Even so, being ethical is much more than doing what feels good or what is expedient—as, unfortunately, some in the philanthropic professions seem to conclude. Confused by the many, often conflicting considerations about what is right, we typically seek refuge in a kind of moral relativism where, we persuade ourselves, every decision is justifiable. Without the use of durable principles and the frameworks for applying them, our actions, whether as human beings or as volunteers and professionals, are quite simply without justification.

In chapter 4, I will focus on and apply these classical lessons, in practical ways that address adequately if artfully the ethical issues to which we in our various philanthropic roles are exposed.

The first need, however, is to *heighten moral awareness*, to more readily recognize an ethical issue when it presents itself. As proposed in chapter 3, one way to develop the moral vision for discerning the tensions and stresses so characteristic of ethics is to consider a range of issues and cases that are representative of our work particularly as fundraisers—issues that begin to exercise our moral muscles with the ethical frameworks designed to develop and strengthen them.

Three   Issues of Consequence and Intention

> A winner tries to judge his own acts by their consequences, and
> other people's acts by their intentions; a loser gives himself all
> the best of it by judging his own acts by his intentions, and the
> acts of others by their consequences.
>
> —Sydney J. Harris[1]

Choosing the right course of action from competing or conflicting
principles is tough enough. Deciding which overall framework,
consequentialist or non-consequentialist, to adopt as a consistent
ethical stance can seem downright confusing. But such is the nature of the art of being ethical.

OF CONSEQUENCE AND INTENTION

The distinguished columnist and humanist, Sydney Harris, offers
an intriguing juxtaposition of "winners and losers," each combin-
ing the classic ethical frameworks popularly identified as *consequence* and *intention*. He seems to suggest that appraising a person's
ethical actions is really a mix of dispositions: "winners" are critical of the consequences they have brought about, and charitable
about the intentions of others; "losers" tend to credit only their
own intentions, and fix critically, judgmentally, on the consequences of others' acts.

That is, even prior to adopting a particular framework there
is, for those who would be ethical, a proper and an improper
stance—a readiness for self-examination and charity toward
others. It seems like a sensible, altruistic disposition, particularly
for those who understand that ethics demands thoughtful choices.

However, Harris's combination of consequence and intention
also suggests that one's framework for ethical judgment need not
be an either/or, either Kant's rational will or Mill's beneficial results. In fact, they may be parts of a common outlook.

46

Harris's play on these frameworks reminds us that ethical behavior has three components: intention, act, and consequence. Each is important to the whole, though each contends for the dominant emphasis. The emphases of Kant and Mill are perhaps most common; but one could also argue that the act is most important in at least one ethical framework, for example among existentialist thinkers such as Sartre and Kierkegaard—perhaps even the American pragmatist William James (1842–1910)—where neither rational will nor beneficial result is as validating for the moral life as passionate decisiveness, as with Kierkegaard's "leap of faith," in crucial but unclear situations.

Are the ethical frameworks for rationally prescribed intention and beneficial consequence compatible, as Harris seems to suggest? As noted in the previous chapter, they are certainly not compatible when it comes to how we justify our acts. However, by calculating an action to result in the greatest good for the greatest number, Mill's intentions are guided by what as a rule people want. And by acting with rationally guided duty, Kant would be happy if good consequences followed. Yet, to Kant, if the consequences turn out badly, the act nevertheless may be ethically justified, though it may not have been prudent or expedient. To Mill, if the consequences are bad, the good intentions one had are simply attributed to poor judgment or represent an exception to the experience of what is generally best for most people. Neither Kant nor Mill, however, simply pits good intentions against good results.

In Harris's subtle "game of life" metaphor, what he (and we) may suspect is how easy it is to be self-serving about our perspective. We may lie about our intentions in order to maintain a posture of rational good will and innocence and deny responsibility for actions that go wrong. Or we may dishonestly claim responsibility for the good results of our actions even though we did not really plan for them.

Still, if posturing and prevaricating about one's intentions or their consequences are morally repugnant to us, being conscientious about the resolution of a difficult ethical issue will likely strike us as reasonable. For some, the fact that one is conscientious about the decision may suffice to justify it.[2] That is, in cases in which it is not very clear to us what the right course of action would be, it is tempting to suppose that what we should do is whatever we conscientiously conclude we should do. Concluding this, however, is open to serious question, if one considers an analogous situation, involving professional judgment.

Suppose that a physician is confronted with a puzzling case. The diagnosis is not in question, but how to treat the patient—to take the medically right course of action—is problematic. The physician prescribes a drug which has seemed to be the most effective in similar cases. But the patient reacts badly and slips into a worse condition. No amount of general competence and conscientiousness could make the prescription the medically right course of action. They may exonerate the physician, but if the prescription made the patient worse, it is not true that the doctor should have done what he decided he should do. Similarly, in ethical matters, it is possible with the best intentions in the world to miss the mark.

It may be disappointing to find that if we turn to philosophers like Mill and Kant for clues concerning the ethically best course of action in troubling situations, we may be pulled in more than one direction. The fact is that the disagreements between formalists and consequentialists reflect stresses that show up in ordinary life. That promises ought to be kept is good; but the consequences of doing so—to self and others—might well be bad. Doing the right thing is not always a clear choice, but it is no less essential to the art of being ethical that we seek the clarity to do it.

PRACTICAL ISSUES

To be ethical exacts a certain price. Fortunately, nonprofit volunteers and professionals are rarely confronted with life-threatening ethical dilemmas, such as Abraham's decision to take his son's life as God commanded, or to lie to protect a fellow hostage from torture or death. Nonetheless, doing the right thing, such as blowing the whistle on the unethical behavior of a superior, or refusing to be party to a conflict of interest can be costly.

However, practitioners more often agonize about situations with something less at stake, though no less vital ethically. Having a simple but generally effective process for addressing these cases will be helpful. Once we have in mind what it means to think and act ethically, and have adopted the governing framework we find most compelling (chapter 2), we should consider a process for ethical decision-making. Discussed and applied in greater detail in chapter 4, such a process should answer three questions:

1.   What seem(s) to be the ethical issue(s); that is, what does one judge to be right or wrong in this situation?
2.   What action(s) would seem to make the situation right; that is, what ought one to do?
3.   What ethical principle(s), and ultimate governing framework, would justify the action(s)?

Before examining this process, we must address a prior task. The first problem for many, especially inexperienced practitioners, is to recognize an ethical issue when it arises. Combined with the lessons of preceding chapters, the best way to become more discerning and self-conscious about matters of ethics in philanthropy is to review the kinds of issues those in the profession most frequently encounter.

The study by the Independent Sector, noted in chapter 1, provides a useful three-tiered classification of responsible action together with examples of issues for nonprofits: (1) obeying the law; (2) doing the right thing, even when tempted for various reasons not to; and (3) wanting to do the right thing, but not knowing how to resolve apparently conflicting obligations.

Consistent with these tiers, but with primary attention to (2) and (3), a review of typical ethical issues for practitioners suggests there are two major kinds of decision-making: (A) drawing lines, often to avoid potential abuse; and (B) making difficult choices, to resolve cases of competing or conflicting alternatives.

The issues seem to fall into two general kinds of actions exemplifying a number of typical ethical tensions, as follows:

Actions affecting donors/prospects; for example:
- o misusing donor funds
- o divulging donor/prospect information
- o giving prospects false information

- o intruding on private affairs
- o exploiting relationships for personal advantage
- o displacing charitable intentions with other motives

Actions affecting charities; for example:
- o conflicts of interest
- o improper removal or use of intellectual property
- o negligent security of confidential information
- o altering or destroying records
- o questionable charges or expense for services
- o misusing organizational funds
- o reporting inaccurate or misleading information
- o hiring disreputable consultants or fundraising firms
- o gagging or mistreating the whistle-blower

A review of several issues representing both kinds of actions and decision-making; and an elementary approach to their ethical resolution, by applying simplified versions of the consequentialist (or utilitarian) and non-consequentialist (or formalist) perspectives, are now in order.

As noted above, practitioners regularly face two principal kinds of decision-making: (A) *drawing lines,* often to avoid abuse; and (B) *making difficult choices* among competing or conflicting values. A brief look at (A) and the concept of abuse in matters of philanthropy is first.

MATTERS OF ABUSE

Nowhere perhaps is the tension between beneficial consequences and dutiful intentions more apparent than in cases that bear on the potential for abuse of rules, laws, and privileges. "Abuse" is one of those inherently vague concepts that begs the question of degree: how much, how far? Related strongly to the timeless metaphor of drawing lines, abuse develops out of voluntary but irresponsible action that, as we say, "goes too far"—as when one takes unwarranted liberties with the use of alcohol, drugs, money, discipline, etc. But when do we take "unwarranted liberties"? For example, is the line crossed when our action is likely to result in more harm than good to ourselves or others (consequentialism)?

Or is it already crossed when our decision to act is contrary to what is intuitively, universally right (formalism)? Sadly, in an increasingly litigious society, we seem only too willing to let the courts decide issues that—with moral reflection—we could or should decide ourselves.

Abuse *within* the law, where general parameters are already drawn, is no less puzzling. Such is the case where an individual's or an organization's activity is legal, but to the ethical observer "smells bad." It appears to exploit, manipulate, or take unfair advantage contrary to the intent of the law. Somewhere the lines for what is *ethical*, but not illegal, have been crossed. They are no longer clear, obscured perhaps by the shifting sands of popular culture or the untoward footprints of unqualified self-interest.

An alarming study of the nonprofit sector deserves our attention. In an impressive display of investigative reporting, Gilbert Gaul and Neill Borowski describe the massive abuses that today characterize many nonprofits. *Free Ride: The Tax-exempt Economy* attempts to document a major trend in the last two decades, particularly among large nonprofit organizations, typically hospitals, universities, and religious interests. Contrary to their purpose, the study alleges, they are rapidly becoming for-profit businesses representing huge economic resources.[3] Exempt from taxation, they shift the burden for supporting the general welfare of society unfairly to taxpayers.

Defined in various categories by the IRS, nonprofits are generally tax-exempt, except for the unrelated business income (UBI) they earn. However, according to the authors, the exemption is so well lobbied and so poorly enforced that the UBI declared is miniscule by comparison with the revenues—estimated at $500 billion in 1990. Sheltered by the charitable, educational, or social purposes under which nonprofits are chartered, these huge revenue streams go untaxed. The authors present a mountain of data to show: that the laws relating to nonprofits—1.2 million of them—are vague and in need of reform which Congress, with urging from powerful nonprofit interest groups, regularly avoids; that despite their profitability and endowments, hospitals and universities continue to escalate costs to inordinately high levels; that they do little to fulfill their charitable or educational missions, for example, by admitting a reasonable percentage of the poor and disadvantaged; that while nonprofits with huge assets pay little or no tax, their donors also take charitable deductions on personal and corporate income, so that vast sums that avoid the economy's tax rolls are subsidized by corporate and individual taxpayers; and that the IRS is woefully underfunded and understaffed to challenge what appear to be major ongoing abuses.

The point is, these nonprofit programs may all be quite legal, yet they seem to border on being abusive. Harmful to the public good, they exploit the vagaries of nonprofit, tax-exempt eligibility to great financial and competitive advantage at the expense of the altruistic, charitable, and educational spirit of the law.

While reform on a national scale may be in order, even lesser nonprofits that simply choose not to question the exemption they declare for the promising profit-making enterprises they develop, are equally vulnerable. Theirs is the ethically questionable, though implicit, policy of suppressing the question of compliance, or of presuming there is no need to "open a can of (regulatory) worms."

Other issues also need our attention.

MISUSING DONOR FUNDS

Reputable colleagues report that one of the more prevalent abuses affecting donors is the misuse of contributions for purposes other than those to which donors assume, perhaps naively, they will go. For example, exploiting the fact that most donors give to what they regard as a worthy cause (and rarely question how the funds are used), nonprofits strapped for operating cash may arbitrarily use the funds to cover general operating expenses. Ironically, some nonprofit leaders claim a kind of "moral right" to do so. A nonprofit is almost totally dependent on private contributions, they reason, donors understand this, and would condone the use. The assumption, though false, is that arbitrary use of contributions is justified by the inherent worthiness of nonprofits, independently of an organization's operating efficiency or program effectiveness.

Of course many nonprofits clearly distinguish up front between gifts restricted or designated by the donor, and those left unrestricted by the donor to be used at the discretion of the nonprofit.

To use the former for the latter, without the donor's consent, is a blatant ethical indiscretion. But why? Because of *accountability to the donor*. For the incipient consequentialist, experience shows that it doesn't pay to break a promise. Donors will lose confidence in the organization, the cause will suffer for loss of financial support, and the public good for the greatest number will not be well served. The aspiring formalist will hold that keeping one's promises is a duty; one could not imagine being the exception to the rule, in violation of the fundamental requirement for trust.

DIVULGING DONOR/PROSPECT INFORMATION

A growing area of potential abuse for nonprofit development staffs and volunteers lies in the use of donor/prospect information. The subject cuts across every segment of nonprofit work. For example, some nonprofits sell their donor lists—names and addresses—to other nonprofits, often without the consent or knowledge of the donors. List-selling is legal and presumably not a breach of confidentiality, since it need not include gift amounts, anecdotal personal information or other more obvious invasions of privacy. But is it the right thing to do?

From an ends-justifying or utilitarian perspective there are obvious benefits. The seller receives a fee and thus adds to revenues that aid in offsetting operating expenses, or better, go directly to the nonprofit's educational or charitable objectives; and the buyer's capacity for fundraising is strengthened with the addition of new prospects. Setting aside the issue of the possible impropriety of the nonprofit's for-profit strategy, is there any harm in this that would outweigh the benefit?

The first concern for the duty-dedicated formalist is consideration for the donor, which should be basic to every practitioner's code. How would donors feel about having their names and addresses sold to others? Is it simply a nuisance that adds to their second-class mail, or a matter of greater concern to them? Clearly, it seems right to ask them, to find a way of gaining their consent to the practice—just as it is considerate to alert them that as donors they will be recognized publicly in the nonprofit's newsletter, provided they have no objection.

The ethical tension is that as effective volunteers and professionals we need access to information, often confidential, for cultivation, solicitation, and stewardship of donors and prospects. But the question is how we justify the use of what we learn, whether or not security is breached. Gaining consent from the donor to use everything on record at the office seems unreasonable and unnecessary. A weaker, more prudent measure, for example, might be to presume the consent of donors, barring their overt objection, by noting up front in conspicuous organizational policy the kinds of information one records—and shares.

The ethical practitioner who focuses on what is intuitively obligatory would argue that concern for the donor is a matter of fundamental respect, independently of the consequences—which, by the way, may include the loss of donors and of the confidence they have in the organization. Even if the nonprofit somehow determines that the added revenue outweighs the finding that few donors object to it, denial of even one donor's claim to respect is wrong. Still, the practitioner who counts on good results may point out that donor lists are readily available to anyone who picks up the nonprofit's annual report. To research addresses takes time, but it can be done. Selling the information is merely a service helpful to fundraisers at large, and furthers the nonprofit's interests. What is the right thing to do?

INTRUDING ON PRIVATE AFFAIRS

The most obvious opportunity for intrusiveness lies in the use of telemarketing. The techniques, borrowed from the for-profit world, are a common means of nonprofit fundraising today, often in conjunction with direct mailings—at a reduced, nonprofit postage rate. It is also interesting, as authors Gaul and Borowski note, that while for-profit telemarketers are prohibited by law in some states from calling customers before 8 A.M. and after 9 P.M., nonprofit telemarketers are not. While few nonprofits would exploit this privilege—due to the likelihood of a poor response, if not out of common decency—the question is how far the efforts of fundraisers should intrude on the privacy of homes. Between nonprofit and for-profit calls to the average household today, many citizens would insist that telemarketing has already gone too far.

Still, as aggressive nonprofits know, friendly, well-trained telemarketers can be very effective. The intrusiveness is lessened somewhat when a loyal constituency expects the practice as part of an annual appeal. Nonetheless, as part of their training, telemarketers should be reminded that there is an ethical line between showing respect to the prospect (and gaining it) and aggressively or obnoxiously pressing to get maximum results.

Today, a nonprofit can also do sophisticated market segmentation of prospective donors by buying census-related data containing vast amounts of personal and demographic information.[4] The nonprofit contracts with a fundraising consulting firm to screen potential donors by their financial capacity and affinities. The cost may be too high for smaller nonprofits, and probably of little value where their constituency is well known. For major nonprofits with potential for regional or national appeal, however, the added thousands of new prospects already qualified and ranked to suit the organization's needs can result in impressive, cost-effective gift increases. An increasingly acceptable practice, but where should the lines be drawn to avoid abusing potential donors?

Gaining a prospect's credit information from one of the national credit bureaus via consulting firms is a short next step—one that a fundraising consultant motivated by one's intrinsically ethical duty (formalism) might oppose as an abuse of a person's fundamental privacy rights. Even the benefits-oriented ethicist or utilitarian could argue that prying into a prospect's credit history without her/his consent would probably backfire once the prospect discovered it. As a new, more pervasive fundraising trend, it could make the charitably inclined of this nation considerably less charitable.

Backed by advanced information technology and management, donor/prospect research today is at least as sophisticated as investigative reporting—from which we learned the trade. Nonprofits develop an impressive capacity for gathering intelligence about an individual's potential, even propensity, for a contribution largely from information that is public at libraries and government offices. Like detectives, researchers commonly regard those they initially investigate as "suspects."[5] A suspect's giving history, tax records, compensation, securities, real property, family connections (and disconnections), and business, social, and educational relationships offer the fundraiser ample insight into an effective strategy for making a prospect out of a suspect.

A thorough research function also gathers information that is very private, even intimately anecdotal, not only for paper files but increasingly for computerized records accessible to those with the "need to know"—all in the effort to gain a fundraising advantage. Indeed, researchers and other development officers may gain information that is downright gossipy and potentially defamatory or damaging to the donor, including, for example, drinking habits, drug problems, or tax evasion. The fact is, most major donors/prospects would be amazed and probably shocked at how much is known about them. Unquestionably, nonprofits have a responsibility to exercise great care not only for what is in the file, but also for what may be revealed in unguarded moments in conversation elsewhere.

Should charities allow donors to review the files compiled about them? A poll of researchers once suggested that over half would be willing to show the complete file; a quarter of them would reveal parts, allowing donors to believe they have seen it all (a deception "justified" by arguing that what donors don't know won't hurt them?); and the remainder would either reveal some but explain that other parts are available only to staff, or refuse to reveal anything.[6]

Those who do research for nonprofits are understandably wary of the consequences of their work. Some send requests for information on plain white stationery and have the responses sent to their home addresses. Some, in a practice sometimes followed by investigative reporters, prefer to pay for copies of the information they request by personal check rather than by organizational check. They fear that their work even with records that are public will create donor suspicion and sour the organization's fundraising effectiveness. Others, however, in a show of dutiful principle insist that attempting to conceal the research by using a personal check is dishonest. They hold that "professionalism"—a vague and inadequate substitute for ethical principle—requires them to be up front, that is, open about their work.

Where should researchers draw the line on what is at once sufficient for an effective approach to prospects and sensitive to their privacy? One fundraising consultant and author of a manual on prospect research limits research to four areas: prospects' financial resources, their relationship to the nonprofit, their interests, and those in or related to the organization who know them. With that information, she says, "we're ready to start building a relationship."[7]

Clearly, it is time to acquaint donors with current research methods and to develop ethically justifiable policy for them *before* donor trust is lost. Recognizing this, the American Prospect Research Association has developed standards and a thoughtful code of ethics (see the appendix) to help identify and prevent such abuses with or without clarification from the courts. The choice for the ethical volunteer, development professional, and nonprofit is between practices designed for maximum benefit and minimal harm, and those derived from inherent respect for the personal dignity of every donor and prospect.

EXPLOITING RELATIONSHIPS

Ironically, ethically conflicting or competing interests (a topic warranting its own discussion later) can arise in the course of the very friendships we cultivate with constituents. For example, to avoid compromising the company's business relationships, corporate codes of ethics often have provisions prohibiting employees from accepting or eliciting monetarily significant gifts from clients. These codes need to be respected as valid constraints on a volunteer fundraiser's activity. Though prudent judgment is the rule when doing business in countries with cultural expectations different from our own, corporate codes also caution their employees against offering gifts that border on bribery.

Such concerns are equally applicable to nonprofit fundraising. Accepting a personal gift may not by itself be ethically wrong. But if as utilitarian practitioners we regularly look to the possible consequences of this action, accepting the gift may compromise our judgment as a volunteer or professional (in favor of the donor, at the expense of the organization) and of the generally accepted rule of fair and equal treatment. Independently of possible consequences, the formalist practitioner may point out, fair and equal treatment of persons is always the right course of action. Of course, intentionally eliciting a personal gift seems wrong. It exploits the relationship with the donor to benefit oneself, as the utilitarian may point out. It also implies disrespect of persons, the formalist could hold, by treating donors as a means to our own end, rather than as persons who are ethically an end in themselves.

Suppose the development officer (or substitute an analogous case of a new board member) had cultivated strong friendships with certain major donors in the officer's former position such that, in the language of conflict of interest, there was potential for "undue influence." The situation resembles the opportunity for abuse in lobbying. To guard against it, government agencies require that private consultants who once worked as high-level public servants refrain for a period of years from lobbying the agencies for their new clients.

In the new position, the development officer who is focused mainly on results may use the knowledge and friendship to advantage, impressing her/his superiors immediately by attracting the donor to the new cause, to the benefit of the organization. Or, the officer may encourage the old donor, out of respect for the former cause, to continue to be loyal there. To whom is one accountable? Of course, the cynic will contend that the final decision is, after all, the donor's—which it is, though the decision is certainly influenced if the officer privately encourages the donor to change loyalties, or silently acquiesces to the donor's inclination to favor him.

Undue influence on a will can be blatant. A case occurred some years ago when a medical professional allowed, as the judge put it, "a confusing mixed relationship of professional care, friendship and romantic feelings" to move his elderly patient to alter her will in favor of the institution that employed him.[8] The influence had the effect of establishing a professorship he would assume, and removed the woman's estate from four other charities to which it was originally directed. The judge declared the altered will invalid and redirected the estate to the original charities. Must the courts decide accountability?

In the field of planned giving where, for example, the development officer often counsels prospects, frequently elderly, over a long period of time about the disposition of their life's assets, undue influence can be more subtle. In one noteworthy case a donor not only made a large gift from her estate to the officer's organization, but also, out of gratitude, to the officer himself after he left the nonprofit. The organization reclaimed the gift in a court suit, on the ground that he had elicited it as a staff member while in the nonprofit's employ. The officer insisted that the gift to him was a personal matter and belonged to him. Indeed, the donor apparently wanted to do it.

In what sense, if any, was the development officer ethically abusive? One could say that the donor's gratitude was misdirected, to which the officer acquiesced. To the practitioner of benefit over harm he set a bad example. He exploited his position and the donor's vulnerability to his personal financial advantage, but at a wider, long-term cost to the specific nonprofit organization and to nonprofit efforts in general. An adherent of the Kantian framework would say he *used* the donor, treating her as a means to an end, rather than as a person having a right to shape her own affairs.

Some may agree that the line between enough and too much influence on certain donors is easily crossed, of course, but that the optimum is often beyond one's control. Recognizing that possibility, does the fundraiser have a duty to dissuade the well-meaning donor, in the case above for example, by suggesting the personal gift be directed to another charitable interest of the donor? The strategy is ethically promising, if it comes to that. Before that, however, one could draw the line by being up front with the prospect about one's professional code that prohibits the taking of personal gifts. Again, it is a matter of accountability.

The National Committee on Planned Giving's standards place the welfare of the donor above every other interest—including that of the charity. The standards state that officers "should have no vested interest in the affairs of a prospective donor which could result in direct personal gain or advantage to themselves."[9] Like typical standards, the injunction is morally appealing; but what justifies it? Either this "should" is perceived as generally the prudent thing to do, because the potential harm to the organization outweighs the personal benefit; or it is a matter of proceeding with what is intrinsically right independently of consequences, based on a principle of ultimate respect for individual dignity and welfare.

DISPLACING CHARITABLE MOTIVES

Finally, fundraising, and particularly planned giving, has become vulnerable to an increasingly pervasive and effective influence: the marketing of tax and income benefits at the expense of charitable intent. The gift potential for nonprofits from estate bequests, unitrusts, annuity trusts and the like is, as nonprofit fund raisers recognize, immense.

The fundamental issue is classic: Why do people give? In this country today no doubt many people make annual contributions mainly to reduce their tax liability, and, as active nonprofit workers alert to taxable year deadlines, we are there to help them. Of course millions of people historically have given and continue to give to charity, with no thought other than to respond to a particular need, or out of a profound obligation they feel to be charitable.

Congress provided tax deductions to encourage the charitably minded, basically to support the long-standing tradition of philanthropy in this country, not to create a false motive for giving. As Aristotle and Jesus (who enjoyed no tax incentives) insisted, giving is its own reward and a challenging duty. It is not a way to pass easily through "the eye of a needle." And yet, the promotion and technology of complex planned gift strategies today come very close to being prudent strategies for financial and estate planning, overwhelmingly canted toward the economic advantages of charitable giving.

When planned giving officers counsel prospects about their charitable interests—and underscore the irrevocable nature of the gift—the priority of charitable intent over *wealth-conserving* strategies is less likely to be skewed. As one professional consultant puts it: "For people to consider permanently separating themselves from a significant asset, there must be something more than tax and income benefits. [Rather, there must be] something like a commitment to a cause that is greater than their own personal interests or the world of tax planning and family benefit."[10]

CONFLICTING OR COMPETING INTERESTS

Cases of conflicting or competing interests (the second major kind of decision-making (B) noted above) range over more than one ethical issue. In fact, they affect donors, including grantmakers, as well as nonprofit organizations. (The concept is broadly applied and deserves additional discussion in chapter 5.) Three cases are representative:

First, there is the case in which a director of a corporate foundation was recruited to become a member of a nonprofit's governing board. The nonprofit's interests were doubly served: the director's expertise contributed to the effectiveness of the board, and her presence no doubt influenced the foundation subsequently to make a grant to the nonprofit.

Several questions will occur to the thoughtful practitioner. For example: Was it appropriate for the nonprofit to recruit the foundation director? Was it all right for the director to accept the invitation? Were either the nonprofit's interests or those of the foundation compromised by the relationship? Normally one would question ethically the nonprofit's rather transparent motive in recruiting the director and wonder how the foundation would allow it to happen. Surprisingly, after sharing her second thoughts about the propriety of the relationship with her corporate superior, she was told it was in the foundation's interest to have her remain with the nonprofit, to assure accountability from the nonprofit for the foundation's investment. Assuming the foundation's motive in allowing her to remain is not ethically questionable, would it be unethical had her membership on the board been a condition for making the grant?[11]

A related case of potential conflict of interest occurs in the context of "cause-related marketing," in which a corporation enters into a marketing arrangement with a nonprofit for their mutual benefit. Originally conceived by the American Express Company, the strategy assumes that consumers will buy the products of a corporation that promises to contribute a portion of its profits to charity. The arrangement lends itself easily to consequentialist thinking. It can increase a nonprofit's visibility by giving it access to the corporation's marketing expertise. In turn, the corporation may increase its sales and enhance its image by association with an attractive cause. But there is also potential harm, to both parties. The corporation may select a nonprofit mainly for its sales attractiveness to consumers, not for its effectiveness or need, and thus exploit the charity to increase sales. The nonprofit may jeopardize its mission, public reputation, or future funding by allying itself with one particular entity.[12] Nonprofit decision makers, governed by formalist reasoning independent of the arrangement's possible benefit or harm, are unlikely to agree to a condition that seems inconsistent with the charity's mission or integrity.

A third case has to do with competing rather than conflicting interests. Corporate codes of ethics, for example, typically include a provision that prohibits its employees from divulging or removing intellectual property for use by competitors. The concern is not lost on fundraising.

Suppose the development officer, or a key volunteer, leaves one nonprofit to join another. Is it ethically permissible to use the previous donor information in the new position? (Given the normal capacity for memory, how could one not help but use it?) Or does the information in some important sense "belong" to the former nonprofit?

Realistically the issue may turn on how much and what kind of information one can in good conscience take to use elsewhere. In the poll of prospect researchers noted above, 12 percent said they would take all the information they had gathered, 58 percent said they would take some, and 30 percent would take none. Most would probably leave the written file contents behind, on the ground that the contents are the property of the nonprofit for which they were developed.

For professional fundraising consultants who gather information for many different clients on an ongoing basis, the issue is different. It turns on ensuring that the information provided for one client creates no competitive advantage or disadvantage—say, the capacity to raise funds—to another former or future client. For both professional and nonprofit developers the issue also poses concerns for the confidentiality of what is learned from place to place.

The issue of competitive nonprofit interests is akin to that of using the trade secrets or intellectual property of one business to unfair advantage in a competitive context. Former employees of some corporations may be restricted by contract from competing in the same area of expertise for another company. Typically, alleged cases of unfair or dishonest competition among businesses are settled by lawyers in or out of court.

Unfortunately, donor/prospect information is more difficult to contain. Often what is known by one experienced development officer about major donors or prospects is known by others in the same working area. The lives, means, and propensities of those with charitable potential are common knowledge among veteran officers regardless of the nonprofits they work for. Superior intelligence about funding sources is the lifeblood of fundraising, and an important credential of development professionalism and experience.

Beyond possible legal or policy restraints, the proper use of information is largely a self-enforceable practice, a matter of ethical discipline. The duty-justifying practitioner will assure respect for the donor and one's former nonprofit. For the consequentialist, the ethical challenge is to evaluate the relative advantages and disadvantages of using the information.

NEGLIGENT SECURITY

A common opportunity for breach of confidentiality occurs when staff and key volunteers gather in advance of major solicitations, say, campaign strategy meetings, to rank and rate the financial capabilities of prospects, often peers. Though it is possible and effective in such meetings to use a "silent," anonymously written procedure to qualify prospects, open discussion often results in the most accurate evaluation.

As technology goes, the now ubiquitous "fax" machine, once an instrument of confidential communication, is commonly open to office view. Electronic mail, together with the incredible resources of the Internet system, are increasingly prevalent and accessible through the computerized networks of many development offices, let alone the so-called "information superhighway." In this and even more sophisticated electronic worlds to come, we should take seriously the experience of distinguished former State Department official, educator, and management expert Harlan Cleveland, in *The Knowledge Executive*. In effect, he argues, nothing can be truly secretive or confidential in this age, in Washington or any other place. Information leaks.[13] Has the capacity for communication, along with the potential for intrusiveness, developed so effectively that only the courts can offer protection against invasion of privacy, defamation of character, or loss of reputation?

How ought donor/prospect information to be handled by active nonprofit workers? Sensitively, we may suggest. But what does that mean, and why? Complying with laws that bear on privacy of information, those dedicated to beneficial results may seek all the fundraising advantages the information affords, provided the harm in gaining the intelligence is negligible. Competitive pressures to bring about the nonprofit's "greater good" may seem to demand it. Workers who abide by intuitively derived ethical imperatives will go beyond the law to justify the use of the information on the inherent respect and dignity due the prospect/donor.

To further their claim to be professionals, fundraisers might consider emulating the client relationship that is characteristic of medicine, law, and religion. This would acknowledge that the jeopardy in unwarranted disclosure or careless security of donor/prospect records is more than a matter of embarrassment to all. We would probably agree it is a negligent breach of confidence and, if intentional, unethical. Indeed, at some institutions, breach of confidentiality is grounds for dismissal.

ALTERING OR DESTROYING RECORDS

Negligent security is a major issue, and not only as it jeopardizes privacy and confidentiality. Computer proficiency has given rise to a new species of ethical mischief: the "bugging" of donor information/management systems, not to gain secrets but to alter or destroy computerized records.[14] Hackers develop rogue software with "viruses" and "worms" that can infect or eat stored information, falsifying or systematically destroying valuable if not irreplaceable data.

Virus-detection software, security access codes, and backup programs are minimal means of the protection we try to provide. But what is to prevent a disgruntled management information systems staff person—a specialist increasingly vital to nonprofit development—from creating this kind of mischief? Perhaps only the specialist's moral character, and commitment to the organization's code of ethical professionalism.

QUESTIONABLE CHARGES OR EXPENSE FOR SERVICES

Ordinarily, planned giving officers and other nonprofit specialists are salaried and take no fees from the constituents or clients to whom they provide their services. They are, however, vulnerable to the lure of extra compensation, from opportunities they have that are comparable to the work of fundraising consultants and other independent professionals. As experts in various aspects of nonprofit work, they may on occasion step outside of their salaried positions, with the consent of their employers, to do private consulting.

The nature of compensation for services is a controversial issue. Among consultants, including lawyers and physicians, for example, it is normal to charge a client an established hourly, daily, or fixed project fee for the services rendered. An exception would be an instance where a client seeking damages has no resources; a lawyer may take the case for a percentage of the damages sought. As a rule of compensation, however, such a commission for services is opposed by most fundraising consultants, and is inconsistent with the National Society of Fund Raising Executives' code of ethics. To charge a commission based on the amount of funds raised is generally viewed as unethical by the profession. But why; what is the right thing to do?[15]

The set fee concept recognizes the value of professional counsel independently of the fundraising outcome which, of course, cannot be guaranteed. To contain the costs, the consultant may assess the nonprofit's capacity to raise its needs, prior to the attempt, and be paid a fee for the study. The consultant's recommendations may vary from a decision to proceed to one that terminates the project. If hired to proceed, the consultant's fee for services is set in advance and will be the same regardless of the amount ultimately raised, based on the consultant's time and expertise. Ultimately, the burden for what is appropriate expense rests on the professional's integrity and competence, and on the nonprofit's considered judgment of the risks and affordability.

However, the commission concept may seem preferable in at least two ways. It provides the consultant with contractual incentive to raise as much as possible, to the benefit of the nonprofit, and it offers the nonprofit a guarantee that its fundraising costs will not exceed a fixed percentage of the funds raised. The commission idea is particularly tempting to the many small nonprofits that are caught in the vicious circle of having no funds with which to pay the consultant to raise the funds they do not have. To make it even easier, the consultant may offer the nonprofit a choice: fee or commission.

From an ethical perspective the commission is seen by some consultants as a way of keeping the profession honest. The consultant is paid only if she/he produces, and only a percentage of that; there is no temptation to raise only enough money to pay the fee. Those who charge fees, on the other hand, note that some donors and grantmakers dislike or restrict having their gifts effectively discounted by the commission. In a major campaign a fee structure is more cost-effective, they claim, and if fees are paid from receipts (preferably unrestricted), that should be understood and approved up front by the nonprofit's board as the most reasonable cost of doing business.

Is it ever ethically *inappropriate* to take a fee?

A few years ago the chief development officer of a major university took a large fee, without objection from the institution, for serving as co-executor of a friend's major estate gift to the university's foundation. An audit showed nothing illegal, hence the action apparently complied with the state's "ethics law." Staff members chose not to testify about the case, perhaps for fear of losing their jobs.

While no policy forbade it there, officers elsewhere are uncomfortable with this practice. They note: (1) a fee for services carries a contractual responsibility at least as compelling as the professional relationship between a salaried development officer and an individual donor and hence is open to potential for exploitation or partiality, if not suit; and (2) even without a fee, as executor and friend there is potential for undue influence over a decedent's will. In fact, some colleges forbid its officers to be executors of estates. On the other hand, an institution's foundation governing board, by virtue of its autonomy ("at arm's-length") and fundraising purpose, might well expect its officers or committees to execute estate gifts, without conflict of interest.

Should a nonprofit pay a "finder's fee"?

Apparently it depends in part on the finder's position. The salaried nonprofit planned giving officer represents a specific philanthropic mission, yet offers charitable gift advice that is the common property of every estate planner and financial advisor. Guided above all by the charitable intent of the prospective donor, the officer's job is to acquaint the prospect with the various kinds of planned or deferred gifts, and to recommend those best suited to the prospect's circumstances.

Often the officer teams up with for-profit advisors to the prospect—accountants, lawyers, trust officers—whose services justify a fee, though they may also work pro bono as volunteers on behalf of the nonprofit. Professionally, their philanthropic service is tangential only; their first priority is to protect the client's legal and taxable interests. It seems reasonable to expect that if the nonprofit seeks the services, it pays the fee; if the prospect initiates the help, the prospect should pay.

Then there is the for-profit financial planner, whose first concern is to maximize the client's assets, for a fee. The planner advises clients how to invest or dispose of their resources, and has no philanthropic obligation other than to take into account the financial advantages of a charitable gift.

Clearly, financial planners, accountants and lawyers are often in a position to recommend such tax-deductible gifts to their clients. As paid professionals, it is part of the service. If the client has no particular charitable preference, the advisor may offer some suggestions—avoiding undue influence—for the client's further consideration, and aid in making the gift.

But there is also the entrepreneur—perhaps a fundraising consultant—who, knowing an individual who is ready to make a major gift, "shops" it and "delivers" it for a fee to the highest nonprofit bidder. Should the nonprofit bid for it?

In principle it may not be a questionable decision provided the fee can be justified in the fundraising budget, perhaps in lieu of hiring a full-time staff to cultivate and deliver such gifts. The idea of marketing a major gift for the best offer is somewhat distasteful to and incongruous with the ideals of philanthropy and puts the nonprofit "haves" at a distinct advantage over the "have-nots." Nonetheless, the would-be consultant seems to provide a valuable service.

Or has the consultant done right by the donor? Only, we might insist, with the prospect's informed consent, for example on the ground that it is also a service—presumably *pro bono*—to the donor as well as the charity. But that is difficult to justify when the service is already free and competent at many nonprofits. The consultant might be on firmer ground, for example, by extending the service to include educating the donor regarding charitable gift possibilities, and objectively researching for the donor some of the many nonprofit causes he/she might support.

Again, it is a matter of serving the best interests of the charity and the charitably inclined, either as a conscientious utilitarian, by weighing the various advantages and disadvantages that generally follow from a proposed action, or as a thoughtful proponent of formalism, by recognizing at the outset the priority of the donors' welfare.

GAGGING OR MISTREATING THE WHISTLE-BLOWER

Finally, one of the most personally agonizing cases of conflict is that of the whistle-blower,[16] a situation developed compellingly for moviegoers in "Silkwood" over the issue of a plant that exposed its employees to life-threatening amounts of radioactive materials. At a level less life-threatening but no less serious, consider the following:

An assistant in a nonprofit's development office learns that her superior, the development officer, has recommended that the organization mount a special fundraising project, contrary to a feasibility study in which the assistant participated. Perplexed by the decision, she challenges the officer in private. He tells her in effect to forget about it, that the decision is not hers to make. Besides, he insists, the organization needs the effort for its own good.

She is troubled: should she report her discovery to the nonprofit director? The officer's recommendation is dishonest, clearly contradicting the confidential comments of key donors—who, however, could be wrong. In one way, she reasons, remaining silent represents no personal injury to her; however, the organization and its constituents may be affected adversely by an appeal that goes badly. (Whether she should reason as a consequentialist or a non-consequentialist is left to the reader.)

She decides to reveal her discovery to the nonprofit's director who, after wondering how to handle it, confronts the officer in private. The officer insists his recommendation is well supported by his own notes. More likely, he argues, the assistant—who is "kind of a troublemaker"—has misrepresented his interview reports. It is time to let her go, he suggests; her services will not be needed on the proposed project. The director reluctantly agrees.

Deeply hurt that doing the right thing has resulted in an injustice to her, the former assistant sues the organization, and the court rules that her position be restored. (Indeed, some states now have statutes designed to protect the whistle-blower.) The hard question is: Has her ethical stance been rewarded? Apparently not. She cannot imagine herself returning to work in an organization she has embarrassed; nor will she be likely to find comparable employment elsewhere in the community, given her reputation as a "snitch" and a possible troublemaker. Her entire career is in jeopardy. Thus, it appears to be a "no-win" situation. Is something wrong in the moral order of things when by being ethical the burden of guilt and general disapproval shift from the wrong-doer to the right-doer?

The preceding cases are only representative, a sampling of the issues, kinds of decision-making, and governing frameworks that confront practitioners in philanthropy.[17] As we shall see in the chapters that follow, developing and applying ethically justifiable policies, principles, and codes exact a serious, often puzzling, and appropriately artful effort from nonprofits, their volunteers and professionals.

It is now time to gather the ethical principles of greatest moment to practitioners and to explore their application to the issues experienced by the "Hospice of Pine Elbow."

Four   Principled Action

If the classical ethicists are right, it takes principled action as well as character worthy of human capacity (with or without divine support) to do the right thing. To that end we should adopt the most promising ethical framework or stance for consistently guiding our actions; identify the norms or principles that justify decision-making for practitioners working in philanthropy; and finally, apply and embody the principles in action.

A CHOICE OF FRAMEWORKS

Ethical frameworks can seem rather complex if one considers the variants and analyses of ethical theory developed in the academic journals. Indeed, the veteran practitioner may require and develop increasingly sophisticated reasoning to do the ethical thing consistently. For all, however, a mastery of the basics, powerful and useful in their own right without further embellishment, should be paramount.

Setting aside the existentialist's leap of faith, noted in chapter 2, two basic frameworks seem most compelling at the secular level: (1) the utilitarian—or consequentialist—stance, in which actions are morally justified by the surplus benefit over harm that most people are likely to experience; and (2) the formalist—or imperativist—outlook, in which actions are ethically justified when they are consistent with what is thought to be intrinsically, universally right. Both frameworks seem to promise personal well-being and character development, though each may define the human condition in a different way. The choice of governing frameworks or moral stances is a matter of what one in general finds most persuasive. Having decided, the task is to be consistent and avoid hypocrisy.

Each framework represents a distinctively different way of justifying ethical action. Yet, the classic rules or principles that support these stances are comparable. For example, both ethical positions promulgate specific principles or rules, such as truth-telling, promise-keeping, and justice. The difference is that for the utilitarian the rules are grounded in experience. If you tell the truth, keep your promises, or show fairness, good things generally happen. For the formalist, the rules are grounded in reason. Telling the truth or keeping one's promises is an unqualified obligation or duty, and is good for its own sake independently of what happens.

Unfortunately, neither framework is very clear or satisfactory for resolving certain ethical dilemmas in which two different and conflicting rules seem to stymie right action. Thus, when telling the truth would jeopardize the welfare of other persons, both the utilitarian framework and the formalist perspective can be puzzling. For example, by holding to the governing principle for doing the greatest good for the greatest number, the utilitarian has an interesting problem. If both truth-telling and concern for the welfare of others are the right thing to do—each justified by the prospect of bringing greater benefit than harm—then applying the same justifying principle for choosing one over the other seems redundant. Resolving the puzzle appears to depend on some other, non-utilitarian way of thinking. In fact some ethicists have suggested that the solution at that point is to become a formalist, and choose the course of action implied by the principle that seems intuitively right!

The formalist also has a problem. Faced with the conflict of truth-telling and the welfare of others, each of which is one's duty, one seems forced to prioritize them. We might reason, for example, that telling the truth is the right thing to do regardless of the consequences to others' welfare. Or, by making a single rule to cover the conflict, it diminishes one's duty. That is, in a case where truth-telling seems pitted against the welfare of others, then assuring the latter by telling a falsehood may be justified as prudent, but it seems quite unformalist to regard it as moral, or to resolve the conflict by applying the utilitarian principle. The existentialists may be right after all; neither experience nor reason seems quite adequate for making some of life's decisions.

To the practitioner prepared to choose between the utilitarian and the formalist perspectives, one difference may be telling. If one believes that the ultimate welfare of the individual is more important than that of the majority, then one is most likely to favor classical formalism. Ironically, even the case of the individual who, as we say, makes the "ultimate sacrifice" for the welfare of others—which could be construed as a utilitarian perspective—seems to underscore the formalist-like premium we place on individual dignity and worth.

PRINCIPLES OF ETHICS IN PHILANTHROPY

Happily, either of the major governing frameworks will serve to justify most decisions practitioners in philanthropy will have to make. Indeed, as we noted, both frameworks will support and ultimately justify comparable ethical principles. So, the next task is to identify a set of primary ethical principles or guides to right action that, governed by one's framework, will help to distinguish responsible from irresponsible decision-making in one's day-to-day work. Later, we will test this set for adequacy and completeness in actual as well as hypothetical cases.

The principles and decision-making procedures that follow are intended mainly as guides, albeit reliable, to ethical reflection in matters of philanthropy. As guides they are basically heuristic; that is, they serve as exploratory probes for discovering which one will most likely discover the right thing to do. They should elicit discussion, refinement, and ethical artfulness. Clearly, they are derived from the discussion of key ethical concepts in the preceding chapters.

SPHERES OF ETHICAL INFLUENCE

For practitioners serving philanthropy's various roles, three ethical domains—although they are not unique to philanthropy—seem to be dominant: *respect, beneficence,* and *trust.* That they are "dominant" need not mean they have ethical priority over related principles, for example, to resolve possible conflicts among principles. Rather, one might compare their relative place to that of the fifth note—the dominant—in a musical scale, or to a planet's gravitational capacity for holding its moons in orbit. Their "sphere of influence" is greater.

Consistent with long-standing human experience, these dominant principles, along with those which seem related to them, form a kind of moral order of thinking. One may decide that the dominant principles of the classical ethicists are written into the universe, in some metaphysical, logical, or scientific sense, but ethical principles need not be laws of nature to be compelling. What we do claim is that they are *spheres of enduring ethical influence*, durable and applicable to the human condition, and, thus, compelling guides to responsible behavior.

For our purposes, the belief in equal ethical regard for every person, a formalist bias, is assumed in this moral order. To think and act in an ethically responsible manner, the following order of things can give conceptual support to one's practical efforts at principled action:

Respect

Respect for persons entails a thoughtful view of self-respect. Proper self-respect or self-worth is based on convictions about human capacity and willingness to do the right thing. The normative (and heuristic) statement of the principle of respect might take the form: *Respect the essential worth and well-being of every person.*

Three closely related ethical concepts, each influential in its own right, lie within respect's sphere of influence and serve to amplify the dominant principle, and to give it applicable value:

(a) *Autonomy:* Regard every person as an autonomous agent, free to determine his/her own destiny; treated as an end, not a means to an end, no person either capable or incapable of responsible decisions should be exploited.

(b) *Privacy:* Accord every person the right to privacy and confidentiality in their affairs, save with their consent or the requirements of law for disclosure.

(c) *Protection:* Assume for oneself and encourage in others the responsibility to protect the worth and respect due others, with a readiness to limit actions that may jeopardize persons' well-being.

Beneficence

Beneficent behavior is of paramount importance for fundraisers, volunteers, grantmakers, and the charitably inclined. The normative form of the principle can be quite simple: *Develop beneficence.*

In its sphere of ethical influence there are two related rules or norms that serve to undergird the philanthropic mission of the nonprofit sector:

(a) *Serving the Good*: Advocate, support and serve worthy altruistic interests, the welfare of others, and the goal of a greater public good.

(b) *Charitable Intent*: Ensure the worthiness of charitable motives and volunteer efforts above other purposes that may serve personal and organizational interests.

Trust

This fundamental principle underscores the centrality of ethical relationships to philanthropy. It essentially takes the form: *Build enduring, trustworthy relationships.*

We can identify five related rules:

(a) *Truth-telling*: Communicate, convey, and record information truthfully, accurately, and completely; avoid misleading or deceiving.

(b) *Promise-keeping*: Make and keep promises, agreements, and contracts that are consistent with organizational purposes.

(c) *Accountability*: Be accountable for the stewardship of donated and organizational resources, and be open to scrutiny by appropriate constituents.

(d) *Fairness*: Seek fairness and objectivity in arrangements that require the sharing of benefits and burdens, privileges and responsibilities.

(e) *Fidelity of Purpose*: In all relationships, be faithful to bona fide professional and organizational purposes; avoid or disclose apparently conflicting interests, inconsistency, and hypocrisy.

At the outset, ethically responsible thinking and acting require that we clarify the ethical issue at hand—by establishing the facts, by attending to the way language and concepts are used, by examining our assumptions, and by being objective, open-minded, and reasonable.

We also underscored the need and capacity for justifying the ethical judgments we make by consistently deriving them from enduring ethical principles or rules such as trust and promise-keeping. These rules, in turn, are governed by the ethical framework we adopt, variously identified for our purposes as the consequentialist, utilitarian, benefits-justifying outlook; or the non-consequentialist, formalist, duty-justifying position.

With these fundamentals in mind, we can now develop a process of decision-making for taking the right course of action. As noted briefly in chapter 3, the process could be guided by three general questions in the following order:

(1) What seem(s) to be the ethical issue(s); that is, what does one judge to be right or wrong in this situation?

(2) What action(s) would seem to make the situation right; that is, what ought we to do?

(3) What ethical principle(s), and ultimate governing framework, would justify the action(s)?

Before describing this model in detail, however, we will look at two alternatives, developed by other writers.

A related process, particularly helpful for weighing the available options for action (as in (2)), is offered by Marilyn Fischer on behalf of the Ethics Committee representing the Miami Valley of Ohio chapter of the National Society of Fund Raising Executives. Often, according to Fischer, we encounter apparently conflicting responsibilities. She believes "there is no single formula which, if applied correctly, will yield an 'ethically correct' decision. Instead, ethical decision-making is a matter of interweaving ultimate concerns with the facts and considerations of a particular situation."[1] Faced with an ethical decision, the practitioner can evaluate the options by answering key questions that represent the major areas of concern for the nonprofit:

Organizational mission: Does a particular option promote or detract from the organization's mission and values? And how does it affect those who ultimately receive the services?
Relationships: Does the option promise to strengthen long-term relationships with colleagues and constituents?
Personal integrity: Does the option encourage or discourage one's personal ethical development?

The strength of this model is its usefulness for clarifying and evaluating one's responsibilities. However, the model reflects an essentially utilitarian or consequentialist framework, by weighing the likely effects of each option against three general standards of what seems good for the organization, its constituents, and practitioners. The process does little or nothing to alert practitioners to non-consequentialist or formalist decision-making, a framework they ought to consider. Moreover, by assuming that "philanthropic virtues such as compassion, benevolence and social responsibility" are sufficient to assure the right decision, the model does not really enable the thoughtful practitioner to discern and apply the ethical principles and rules that might justify one's actions. Nonetheless, for those who adopt a utilitarian-like framework, the model may be very useful, particularly as it enables the organization to identify the most compelling option for responsible action.

Ethicist Kenneth Goodpaster provides his students in business ethics with a very useful "template" for analyzing ethics-related cases.[2] More comprehensive and thus open to other frameworks than the Fischer model, it can be very helpful to the practitioner as she/he becomes more discriminating in the analysis of ethical "outlooks" or ways of thinking.

As noted in chapter 2, the template enables the student to locate one's moral stance among four major kinds of ethical thinking: (1) interest-based (e.g., utilitarian), (2) rights-based, (3) duty-based (e.g., formalist), and (4) virtue-based (e.g., Aristotelian). One's outlook is revealed by analyzing a particular ethics-related situation in five steps:

Describe how the situation came about, what the key issues are, and who the key stakeholders are. Identify the interests, rights, duties, or virtues that are evident.

Discern what appears to be the most important issue. Note if there are conflicts or tensions among the interests, rights, duties, or aspects of character that are evident.

Display the principal options for deciding a course of action.

Decide on the best option to take, based on one's considered judgment.

Defend your course of action and note the "outlook" that seems to be predominant in your choice of options.

Both of these models nicely complement and amplify the process we offer below. The Fischer model helps to clarify the alternative responsibilities that may be at stake for the organization; the Goodpaster template illuminates the major ethical outlooks one might adopt. Consistent with preceding chapters, the process that follows is designed mainly to develop in the practitioner an increasing capacity for justifiably principled action.

Once again, recalling what it means to think and act in an ethically responsible way (chapter 2), consider the following steps when addressing a case or situation (chapter 3) that seems to demand an ethical course of action:

(1)   *What seem(s) to be the ethical issue(s); that is, what does one judge to be right or wrong in this situation?*

We noted in chapter 3 that practitioners in philanthropy commonly confront two kinds of decision-making: (A) drawing lines, often to avoid abuse; and (B) choosing between competing or conflicting courses of apparently desirable action.

Typically, we may be inclined to take some action (x) which we are aware may be morally right or wrong. We then clarify the situation to reveal the moral tension in it. Initially, for example, the tension is as simple as: Should one do (x) or not? However, upon reflection the situation—and the question—is often more complex, representing tensions between different possible courses of action.

Among kinds of decision-making, an example of (A)—line-drawing—would occur when one is tempted to exploit a close relationship with a donor to gain a personal objective. An example of (B)—conflicting courses—would be having to choose between a sure and desperately needed grant on the condition the organization agrees to the corporate funder's marketing plan and the uncertain pursuit of a grant from other potential funders, with a proposal that is more consistent with the nonprofit's mission and objectives, with no strings attached. (For help to further identify and analyze the issues, ethical tensions, and options for action, see the Fischer and Goodpaster models above.)

(2)   *What action(s) would seem to make the situation right; that is, what ought one to do?*

In (A), the case of the close relationship, we may decide we ought to refrain from using friendship, gained under professional circumstances, to achieve a personal favor; and instead, to cultivate the relationship above all to serve the organization. Or, to gain a personal advantage that may never come again, we may feel an exception in this case is worth the professional risk. In (B), the grantseeking example, a case for the right action might be made for either choice presented under (1), particularly if the corporate grantmaker's conditions seem ethically acceptable to the organization. Reflecting on the set of ethical principles above, is there a relevant ethical domain or sphere of ethical influence that would guide and justify our decision and make it ethically worthy?

(3)   *What ethical principle(s), and ultimately governing framework, would justify the action(s)?*

At this point we attempt to draw on the ethical principles and rules we have already applied to philanthropy. For example: Under which of the *dominant* principles or spheres of ethical influence does the issue seem to fall? Is it influenced by one or more of the principles of respect, beneficence, or trust? Which of the *related* rules or principles—there may be one or more—in that sphere of ethical influence, might serve to focus and initially justify our proposed action(s)?

In (A), the example of the close donor relationship cited above, respect for the donor is an evident primary principle or dominant sphere of ethical influence. Specifically, it suggests the closely-allied principle relating to *autonomy* and the wrongfulness of exploiting persons. Acknowledging that this is generally true, the practitioner nonetheless may decide that making an exception in this case will do no lasting harm. However, we might also draw on the primary rightness of building trustworthy relationships on behalf of our organization. More to the point, we might invoke the related principles of *accountability* and *fidelity of purpose*. If pressed to invoke a governing framework, the utilitarian practitioner may sense that to use the friendship is more harmful than beneficial in most cases, including this one. The formalist practitioner will note the intuitively rational necessity for individual respect and trust in all human relationships (no exceptions) as the framework that takes precedence over the utilitarian assessment of consequences.

In (B), the grantseeking example, some in the organization may favor accepting the terms of the grantmaker's offer on the grounds that it promises several financial and promotional benefits for the immediate future. Others may prefer pursuing a grant that, however uncertain, would clearly further the nonprofit's mission and long-term objectives.

The choice of these alternatives should be influenced first by the dominant principle for developing *beneficence* and, more specifically, by the related principle urging the single-mindedness of *charitable intent* over other interests. However, we should also consider the dominant principle of *trust*, particularly the related rule of *fidelity of purpose*. Our ethical framework provides the ultimate justification of the choice we make. The formalist practitioner will appeal to the intrinsic duty, independent of other motives, to pursue beneficent and trustworthy relationships. The practitioner who looks primarily to what is beneficial for the organization and its constituents will weigh the relative advantages and disadvantages of the alternatives, consistent with the principles of beneficence and trust.

Of course the real-life situations we encounter are often more demanding, the differences more subtle, the choices more difficult than the hypothetical cases just discussed. As noted at the start, drawing ethical lines and choosing the right course of action among competing alternatives demand artful reflection, a capacity developed and refined, according to Aristotle, over a lifetime of thoughtful decision-making. Nonetheless, consistently acting from durable ethical principles is a good bet for taking right and justifiable actions. However uncertain, halting, or mistaken one's decisions are at times, principled action is accountable action, and a time-honored way to define and develop both personal and organizational character.

The following hypothetical case depicting ethical concerns encountered in what we hope is an atypical nonprofit may help to show the practitioner how the models, ethical frameworks, and principles noted above can be brought to bear.

THE HOSPICE OF PINE ELBOW: A CASE STUDY

Hospice care for the terminally ill has grown rapidly in the last two decades. From a handful of programs in the seventies, there are today approximately 2,000 in the United States, that as yet care for only a small portion of the estimated 250,000 who suffer with incurable ailments. Their numbers are growing by more than 20,000 annually. While 80 percent of Americans die in hospitals surrounded by impersonal life-support systems and the care of professionals they hardly know, hospices offer the friendly dignity of a home or dedicated shelter, at a cost that is dramatically lower than a hospital. With Medicare and Medicaid the average daily cost to the patient without private insurance is minimal. Many patients have written "living wills" that specify their choice of a hospice, and nursing care is used mainly to relieve the patient's final pain.

Like many nonprofits, the Hospice of Pine Elbow is seen as an important and unique community resource, but it struggles annually to make ends meet, due in part to inefficiencies in the reimbursement system, and to old high-interest loan payments for purchase, renovation, and maintenance of the facilities.

Established in 1981, it provides the area around Pine Elbow with a combination of residential and in-home care for as many as twenty patients. It is administered by Alice, the full-time executive director; the financial officer, John (also responsible for personnel); Matt, the development officer; Cheryl, Matt's associate for public relations and records, which are computerized as part of a small office network; a part-time director of volunteer services; and 3.5 FTE (full-time equivalent) staff support persons. Beginning with a single house originally given to the organization for the program, the facilities now include four older homes appropriately renovated. One houses the office.

Associated with a large county hospital system, the hospice benefits from health care professionals as needed, and from social and ministerial services of the region. It also depends on dozens of community volunteers, trained in occasional seminars to provide appropriate aid and comfort to the dying and their families. While some in the community doubtless see irony in the organization's acronym (HOPE), to most—especially the dying—it matches their faith in the undying dignity of human life.

The board is fairly typical. Members are people who are willing and able to serve and regarded as reputable and reasonably effective community leaders. They include a long-time family physician, a popular high school teacher and coach, a successful dairy farmer, and a Protestant minister prominent in one of the local service clubs. All are retired. Two are women: one a very active member of other community boards and clubs, and the other a young mother who lost a child to cancer. The males include an attorney with Sefcik, Sefcik & Hagen (SS&H), the largest law firm in the county, which provided a good many pro bono hours drawing up HOPE's nonprofit articles, bylaws, and tax-exempt status; the president of the local S&L, at which the organization banks and carries its facilities loans; and the owner of Pine Elbow Construc-

tion, the newly elected chair of the board who is about to turn
his business over to his son-in-law.

A BOARD MEMBER RESIGNS

There are two vacancies, one by death and one, Mary S., who resigned abruptly and let it be known around the community that
she had differences with the administration over its management
of funds. Actually, she was HOPE's oldest volunteer and "Pine Elbow Volunteer of the Year." A well-known, and some say wealthy,
widow, she was appointed to the board for her long and devoted
service (and the thought that she might one day put the hospice in
her will?). Boundlessly active, she was in the office daily, often to
the staff's discomfort, peering into donor records (how could she
carry out her responsibilities without accurate information?),
copying various items (which no one dared question), walking in
and out of administrators' offices.

The trouble was that Mary was strongly bent on raising funds
in the community—and good at it—for things she felt the hospice
needed. She did this completely on her own, though representing
the hospice, and often without the staff's knowledge. It was hard
not to be grateful.

Of course, her personal campaigns also created problems for
the annual fund and added to John's accounting requirements. A
novice sculptor and long-time patron of the arts, Mary offered to
do a statue depicting HOPE's mission. She said she would need a
few thousand dollars for materials and studio setup, but she would
contribute her skill (and write the project off as a charitable tax
deduction). The board carefully tabled her offer, as John recommended, for lack of discretionary budget funds.

Later, based on several complaints from confused donors, John
suspected she had been soliciting for "an emergency annual fund"
but had told John the checks were designated for "the statue
fund," which he had receipted accordingly. John complained to
Alice that Mary had gone too far this time; she had deceived donors in order to get her statue funded!

Alice was troubled by the situation and wondered if and how it should be reported to the board. She regretted the fact that HOPE had developed no standards or code to address such matters, but, she decided, this was not the time to do it. She wanted no difficulty just now when her contract was about to be renewed. To avoid embarrassment, she thought, she need not mention it to the board, but maybe the organization should write donors a letter apologizing for "an administrative error." Clearly, she mused, it was not John's fault; and to say so would be an affront to John, who took his responsibilities seriously. Indeed, she knew, John was no wimp; if his integrity were threatened he could blow the whistle on this situation, sue the organization, and go to the media with the whole messy truth.

Alice told John she would take care of it with the board's executive committee, and she decided John should apologize to donors for the "confusion." That's what it is, she insisted, and no one needs to know what kind of confusion it was. John agreed some kind of letter should be sent, and he would draft it. But how would he explain the need for the letter to Mary, who would find out sooner or later? Perhaps he should casually mention the confusion when she came to the office, hope she finds some plausible way to cover her guilt, and thus avoid a bad scene.

When John tried this approach, Mary angrily responded that donors are fickle, change their minds, then blame others for the confusion. She accused John of doubting her integrity, and she abruptly resigned. Some board members felt John's action was insensitive and even wondered if Alice should fire him. Considering Mary's service to HOPE, the situation could have been overlooked, with regrets to donors handled by phone, and no written record. What will people say? HOPE will certainly never be in Mary's will now. Still, as John noted, how would HOPE record the funds? After an awkward discussion, the board agreed to accept Mary's resignation "with regrets," to feature her soon in the newsletter, and to send her a certificate of appreciation for her outstanding service.

Board members want to fill the board vacancies, but sentiment about the right way to do it is divided. The chair and the banker feel the hospice needs persons of wealth, or at least, as the attorney and dairy farmer urge, those with connections to wealth. How long, they asked, can HOPE continue to run with an operational deficit? The teacher and the minister are together in arguing for diversity, to acknowledge the growing minorities in the area. After all, they reminded the others, diversity is a national concern. The physician, the woman active in community affairs, and the young mother favor adding expertise in the counseling of the terminally ill—maybe an academic from the university whose specialty is death and dying. It would, they pointed out, restore credibility to the program in response to criticisms stemming from a family whose displeasure with HOPE was the recent subject of unfavorable investigative reporting by a local television station.

Commentary

One would judge that Mary is a conscientious volunteer, but she abuses her board position by taking liberties with staff, records, and fundraising objectives. Evidence suggests she has deliberately misled both donors and John, the financial officer. Generally she has broken the fundamental principle of trust, specifically the rules for truth-telling, promise-keeping, accountability for resources, and fidelity of purpose. Alice and others are inclined to overlook it to avoid embarrassment and bad publicity, maybe on the outside chance that John is mistaken. But, they cover up the truth by considering how to mislead donors about the confusion. Perhaps Alice has allowed her fears (job security, whistle-blowing) to color her ethical judgment. Mary, in turn, probably lied about what donors told her, and the board engages in hypocrisy by honoring her service. How should the situation have been handled? The final issue—how to fill the board's vacancies—represents competing notions of what is best for HOPE: adding financial strength, becoming more representative of the community, and improving HOPE's image. Which of these makes the strongest ethical case?

(Note: If practitioners need similar guidance to discern and address the ethical concerns that continue to surface in this case, they should look in the commentary after each situation, as well as to the decision-making models suggested above.)

The executive director, Alice, is well-educated, organized, energetic, and nearing the end of her first contract period. Clearly, she aspires to a position of greater magnitude at some point in the future, but for the present the hospice represents a worthy cause and a challenging set of organizational issues.

Although she and the board have no strategic plan or process, they have two major objectives: to distinguish the Pine Elbow program as a model for hospices in the region, and to achieve financial stability. The basic problem is the lack of discretionary funds for program development and capital needs. To cut expenses Alice has already eliminated two staff positions—her administrative assistant and a part-time computer technician. Without substantial outside funding, expansion is not possible. Except for a last minute appeal at Christmas, promoted as a one-time urgency, the hospice would not have made its last annual budget, and current expenses are ahead of projections once again.

A community focus group helped Alice brainstorm the first objective. Among its best ideas was a plan to add short-term housing accommodations for family members from out of town, a library area for inspirational and professional materials on care for the dying, and conference space that might enable HOPE to become the regional center for the hospice concept.

She drafted a grant proposal with which to approach various foundations for project support. Funding for added facilities or for endowment might have to come from other sources. Matt, the development officer, would design new strategies for increasing private gifts, perhaps a capital campaign. The board agreed with the overall plan.

When Edward, the retired farmer on the board, learned that Alice would approach the InterAg Corporation, a major producer of fertilizer, with a proposal for program support, he saw a chance to use his old political connections for HOPE's benefit. As a former chair of the state legislature's agriculture committee he had been lobbied often by the firm to moderate environmental impact demands. He would apply a little pressure of his own on his friend,

Sterling, an executive with InterAg who also served as its foundation committee chair.

Very cordial and noticeably anxious to help (he needed no reminder of past favors), Sterling pointed out that while new services to expand the care and public awareness of the terminally ill were certainly worthy, and fit the foundation's general categories for social and educational philanthropy, the request was not likely to be among the committee's funding priorities. When Edward asked why, Sterling confided: the foundation director is new and is still working on current grantmaking objectives; but "just between us," the members want programs that foster rural economic development, preservation of the family farm, things like that. "Slant your program toward rural welfare," he suggested, "and I'll see what I can do."

When Edward told Alice to rethink the proposal to reflect what he learned, she inserted a "major objective" asserting that expansion of HOPE's program would enable it to serve "the rapidly growing number of patients from rural areas." Although she had no substantiating data, Alice felt there must be more and more retirees moving to the city from the farm. She sent InterAg the proposal.

InterAg's foundation director called to acknowledge the proposal, though from HOPE's previous requests in the files he concluded the organization was neither financially stable nor well governed; in short, not a good candidate for a grant. To Alice he carefully noted that HOPE's objectives might be somewhat marginal for InterAg's grantmaking program, but he closed by pointing out that of course the final decision would be up to the committee.

Commentary

Various principles of respect (for the worth of others), beneficence (priority of charitable intent), and trust (truth, consistency of purpose, fairness) are in jeopardy. Edward, the farmer/board member, seeks a favor and will, by means of personal, perhaps privileged counsel and untoward influence from Sterling, the executive, probably get it. Thus, the playing field is uneven, unfair to other grantseekers. With the advantage of privileged information Alice has rewritten the proposal to suit the unpublished interests of the foundation committee which Sterling chairs; though in fact her "major objective" to include more rural patients is incidental to HOPE's plan to expand facilities, and thus compromises the board's intentions. The foundation director properly questions HOPE's worthiness for a grant, but is aware that Sterling and the committee have final authority, and that it would be imprudent, however ethical, to challenge it at this time. Did Alice have a better, more ethical course of action open to her?

NEW DEVELOPMENT STRATEGIES FOR HOPE

Matt, the development officer, is new to the organization: young, engaging, ambitious, but inexperienced except for three years in the direct mail division of the local United Way. He is quite capable of directing HOPE's annual fund and, working with Cheryl, his associate (who updates records, helps with mailings, and writes a quarterly newsletter), he hopes gradually to build a more comprehensive development program.

In keeping with his commitment to Alice, he has been attending seminars on various aspects of fundraising offered by the local chapter of NSFRE, and has begun to develop some expertise in planned giving on his own. The current budget does not allow for more intensive training at professional schools or seminars. He knows how to organize and train volunteer solicitors; however, he has never planned or participated in a capital campaign. In fact, neither has HOPE.

Considering the overall plan for HOPE, Charlie, the board chair—who knows what it costs to build nowadays!—feels they will need about $1 million over and above possible program support—about half of that for new facilities to house the proposed center, and the remainder for endowment to help maintain it and the expanded program. He has some *pro bono* estimates from an architect he used to work with—a consideration, he noted, for all the business they had done together over the years. Of course, he added, it's only fair that the architect be invited to bid on the design when the time comes. (In his mind Charlie also included but did not mention the advantage of a construction bid from his own son-in-law.)

As for endowment, Charlie pointed out to the board, it is time to have one, like other nonprofits. William, the banker, agrees. HOPE should be earning its own interest to cover facilities work down the road, once it pays off its loans. Why, he said, there must be a lot of potential for endowment gifts out there—bequests from grateful hospice patients and those they leave behind. He proposed that HOPE develop a brochure that says something like "endowment lives forever" and that Matt should get busy and talk to those patients—and maybe take the minister along. Yes, the lawyer added, and Matt should look into "living wills." They are perfect for our situation; they relieve the family of financial concerns by providing the dying with money for expenses; and by reducing estate taxes encourage the donor to earmark some or all of the residue of the patient's assets for HOPE, upon the person's death.

No one disagreed with these strategies; nor did anyone question whether the community would support them. One member did remind Charlie they would also need to intensify annual fund efforts to meet the budget—and the added costs of a campaign. "That's right," banker William responded; "What will it cost, and how do we pay for it?"

Alice estimated that with a beefed-up phone-mail effort, new promotion and fundraising materials, a few meals and some travel to cultivate major donors, and maybe the services of an experienced campaign consultant for several months, the costs could reach $75,000 or more over, say, a two- to three-year period— added to the current budget. Board member comments followed:

"Surely we can do it for less!"
"Yes, why do we need a consultant? I've been on plenty of church and community fund drives."
"Let's ask the community foundation for expense money; I have a couple business friends on the board."
"I suppose board members could contribute the expense money themselves, but that's a lot of money for this board."

"You bet! I don't know about the rest of you, but I'm on a fixed income, and I think people should figure the time and effort we put into this organization."

"Well, you never know; if we let contracts to the *right* people, we could make up that cost in savings alone."

"Our credit is good; we could borrow expense money from the bank, with pledges as collateral until funds come in."

"For our part, my husband and I could throw a benefit at the club; but our friends would not want their gift to pay for expenses."

"It's a cost of doing business, and we already spend a good 25 percent of our budget on fundraising; so let the consultants raise our funds for us, earn their 10 percent or whatever, as long as we clear a million dollars."

"But what guarantee can we get from the consultant?"

"That's why you hire consultants; besides, we don't have to broadcast what it costs, and people won't ask."

Turning aside Alice's suggestion, the board decided it could do without a consultant. It also agreed to take campaign expenses out of early receipts; after all, someone pointed out, contributions are contributions, so that published reports of total receipts toward HOPE's goal would not really be inaccurate, and would never be questioned.

Commentary

Some of the attitudes suggest poor judgment or the absence of good policy, but not necessarily bad ethical judgment. One might argue, however, that the board has a responsibility to "audit" its practices and policies for ethical consistency and legal compliance, and not least to be more representative in its membership. Clearly, Charlie, the board chair, has exploited a business relationship for his own ends, and thus has challenged the fundamental principle of respect. He also expresses no qualms about possible conflicts of interest (again, the principle of trust); in fact he would probably argue for the advantage of his connections and their self-interests to the organization's good. His beneficence, another fundamental principle, is thus a question, and the board is in danger of actions contrary to principles of fairness and congruent purpose, principles related to trust. Also, side-stepping the concern for disclosure (truthfulness, and trust), the board intends to publish contribution figures that mask fund-raising expenses and avoid accountability for resources—a trust principle—to the public. How should one correct these attitudes and actions, and whose responsibility is it?

A VISIT WITH ALFRED

Julius, a successful entrepreneur originally from Pine Elbow, now retired and living elsewhere, has long shown unusual interest in HOPE. Eighty-three years old, he regularly flies in to visit his close friend and one-time business associate, Alfred B., now a patient at HOPE, and he sends generous contributions on an annual basis. Though the staff has done no hard research on Julius, his estate would surely be in the several-million-dollar range. Some years ago, after his first wife's death, he married his former secretary, a widow of independent means, now seventy-eight and a one-time HOPE volunteer. He has one daughter by his previous marriage, who does not approve of Julius's second wife. She has two grown children, both well-established professionals (thanks to Julius's generous educational support) on the West Coast.

Given the board's rather pointed suggestion, Matt decided on a dual strategy: to visit Alfred and his family in the hospice and ask about his feelings for HOPE; and to begin to cultivate Julius for a major gift, perhaps a bequest by will.

The visit with Alfred might be awkward, Matt thought. The relationship between Alfred and Julius would make it easy to gain Alfred's confidence; but surely Alfred and his family would know Matt was not there solely out of concern for Alfred's condition. Was it disrespectful to the dying to do this? And how should he present himself? Express concern that Alfred's affairs were in good order, to the benefit of his family? Or suggest directly that Alfred consider HOPE in his will? Should he be painfully honest about his purposes? That would be pretty abrupt. No, he would say his primary purpose was to ask Alfred's counsel about approaching Julius for a gift—and hope Alfred would begin to talk about his own intentions. Of course he would note HOPE's need for endowment, the plans to build a center, and the naming opportunities they presented. Then too, there are the tax advantages and, with a will, a way to avoid probate court.

Cultivation of Alfred might take several visits, Matt reflected, and then there is his family, an uncertainty which might present some tricky sensitivities. He had better use the first visit to gain Alfred's confidence, sow the seeds for a charitable gift, and learn as much as possible about Julius from one who knows him intimately. With the right approach, Alfred would tell him a lot about Julius.

Commentary

Matt, the development officer, apparently intends to exploit Alfred's terminal condition to gain intimate information about Julius in the hope of soliciting major estate gifts from both individuals. True, there may be significant charitable advantages to both Alfred and Julius, as well as to Matt and to HOPE. However, Matt would do well to consult the law first regarding the rights of vulnerable classes of persons. In any case, Matt is using Alfred—an abuse of the principle of respect—but he is also hiding his intentions, contrary to the idea of trust, to elicit a gift from Alfred. Is there a problem about using the intimate information about Julius that Alfred reveals? Has Matt properly considered the other sensitivities met with in his approach? Could he make a compelling ethical case for it to the board?

JULIUS'S WILL

With a precarious heart condition that required bypass surgery, Julius, at his wife's urging, drew up a will with the help of his attorney prior to the surgery. In addition, his wife was given power of attorney over the estate in the event of Julius's death.

After a less than satisfactory recovery, he and his wife reviewed estate matters and began to give greater attention to how his assets should be distributed upon his death. He felt that HOPE should be among his charitable interests. He agreed it was time to discuss a bequest with appropriate people at the hospice.

His wife called Matt, explained the interest, but wanted HOPE to handle everything. She did not want to elicit her stepdaughter's already heightened suspicions. A bequest would be a coup for Matt. He felt the simplest proposal would be for Julius to add a codicil to his will, giving HOPE either a fixed amount or a percentage of the estate. Matt called Julius's attorney, noted the wife's wish, and asked the attorney to draw up the codicil and present it to Julius.

The codicil was presented but never signed. Julius's condition worsened, and he had additional surgery and another lengthy if not uncertain recovery. Staying abreast of the situation with Julius's wife, Matt sensed she was worried about Julius's condition but also concerned that the codicil should be signed. She was unwilling to press the issue herself with Julius, who might think she was more interested in the estate than in him. Moreover, under persistent questioning, she had revealed Julius's thoughts about HOPE to her stepdaughter.

Matt called the attorney occasionally to keep things moving. The attorney always advised waiting until Julius was better. Finally he curtly warned Matt to back off. He felt HOPE had already brought too much pressure to bear, and he mentioned something about "undue influence." Matt really did not understand the phrase, but, coming from a lawyer, it frightened him.

Then Julius's daughter called Matt. Her resentment of her stepmother's and Matt's involvement was evident, and she wanted to know everything HOPE knew about her father's plans, including information HOPE already had on his prior contributions and net worth. After all, she insisted, she had a right to know. She herself had contributed to HOPE in the past, but she would certainly reconsider, or do worse, if she did not get the truth. When Matt explained, half truthfully, that he really did not know her father's plans, she accused him of withholding information, interfering in the family's affairs. She suspected HOPE was in Julius's will, and was prepared to contest it.

James, the lawyer/board member, was aware of what Matt had done. He would talk to Julius's attorney and deny there was any undue influence. As for other legal action, James felt Julius's daughter had little basis on which to contest the will, and unless the codicil was signed, the question was moot.

Matt wondered: He and Julius's wife were on good terms; should he now gently persuade her to ask Julius for his signature? Matt might mention that Julius should have the satisfaction while still alive of putting HOPE—where his good friend Alfred was—in his will. Indeed, Alfred should be told of it before he died. The alternative, Matt reflected, was simply to wait and see what happens. If Julius died, maybe his wife's power of attorney would be enough to insure a gift from the estate.

Commentary

Responding to the wife's request, Matt's motives may be mixed, trying to be helpful and hoping for a gift. But he may have crossed the line by pressing the codicil signing issue to the point of interference in Julius's affairs, bordering on undue influence and disrespect. He may argue that it was excusable; however, he also considered how to exploit Julius's condition and friendship with Alfred to influence the signing. Matt cleverly avoided the daughter's demand for (right to?) confidential information, but he might have been more forthright by noting that it would be contrary to HOPE's policy and unethical for him to divulge it. In any case his stand probably cost HOPE any future contributions from the daughter. How might Matt have proceeded more responsibly?

A CORPORATE SOLICITATION

With a small ad hoc committee of the board, Matt also drew up a list of potential major donors in the community. Ranking and rating them for charitable potential was difficult. None seemed a likely prospect for a lead campaign gift, so Matt suggested they test the waters by quietly approaching a few prospects they knew best.

William, the banker, picked the large, locally-owned textile mill, which he knew was doing very well. The owner and he were friends, brothers in a major fraternal organization, and had done a lot of business together over the years. William and Matt arranged a visit with the owner, Marvin. They presented HOPE's plans and needs, and asked Marvin to consider a corporate (and perhaps family) gift in the range of $45,000–$60,000 over three years. Marvin explained he had never been asked for a pledge of cash that large, and felt that it was more than the firm could do out of its profits, although, he admitted, the special tax advantages for corporate gifts would be helpful.

However, Marvin went on, he would consider a smaller, family gift—and maybe also an in-kind contribution of the mill's carpet throughout the facilities, especially in the proposed center, provided the mill could realize some businesslike benefit. Obviously, he noted, the value of the carpet to the project would be substantial, and HOPE would surely need it. But, he reminded William and Matt, he would have to justify the gift to his board (actually his family). Profitability is the "bottom line," good for the community's economy, etc. For example, Marvin suggested, we could have a sort of "partnership." With the right promotion, the mill might increase its sales, and the hospice project would greatly benefit from the firm's marketing prowess throughout the region—itself a costly investment for the mill (TV ads, outdoor signs, perhaps a display of products at the opening day reception). Almost as an afterthought, Marvin conceded the arrangement might also increase the value of the mill's goodwill, against persistent charges in the media ("from a couple of misguided nonprofits") that it was exploiting minority laborers and delaying installation of pollution controls.

They all agreed to get together again at a later date. As they left, William told Matt it was a good deal for HOPE and he would recommend it to the board committee. Thinking to himself, Matt could appreciate the value of the carpet and the campaign marketing, but felt the "partnership" might pose some uncomfortable aspects. Still, he wondered if (how) he should say so to the committee. The gift would certainly strengthen his credentials and put him in good stead with Alice and the board.

Commentary

A case of "cause-related marketing," the principles of beneficence (the primacy of charitable motives), trust (action consistent with one's mission), and respect (for the reputation and worthiness of colleague organizations) seem to be at stake. William, the banker, may argue that the association is good for everybody: the mill is the community's major employer, a boon to the area's economy; the value of the gift and the promotion of the project outweigh, as William said, "the rather tiresome, and I think sometimes irresponsible" charges by nonprofits encouraged by the media. Might there be compelling reasons not to form the partnership? Can he, Matt, and the organization ethically justify the decision?

A LEADERSHIP PROSPECT

Matt and his assistant, Cheryl, regularly review information she gathered on other current and prospective donors. With a tip from James, the board lawyer, one "suspect," whose mother had died at the hospice during the year, stood out. Stephen was a former partner in the SS&H law firm, and related to its founder. James had handled a complex divorce settlement for him. Steve had recently retired at a rather early age and had a permanent home near the racetrack, where he was part owner of several horses. He also owned a condo on one of the offshore islands to which he often flew in his own Learjet. James obviously knew him very well. They were close in age, buddies in law school, often hunted, fished, and partied together, same country club, etc.

Using an assumed name to avoid suspicion, Cheryl gained additional information from the library and the courthouse and promptly stored it, together with the lawyer's insights, on the computer. Public records revealed, for example, that Stephen was a member of several corporate boards, held thousands of valuable stock shares and options, and deeds on assorted parcels of choice undeveloped land on which, however, there were delinquent taxes.

An only child, Stephen also had inherited his mother's estate— large enough, James confirmed, that Stephen would now be looking at ways to shelter the bulk of it from taxes—unless, as Cheryl noted in her report, he had already obligated it in obsessive gambling at various tracks and casinos around the country. Moreover, though an old newspaper story about the sudden increase in illegal narcotics in the area seemed to link Stephen with suspected underworld figures along the southeastern U.S. coast, SS&H had vigorously denied that Stephen and his offshore clients were involved. Matt and Cheryl estimated Stephen's net worth at about $18 million; hence he was a person who could certainly afford a lead pledge of $250,000 or more if properly approached.

As a member of the *ad hoc* committee, James offered to approach Steve, preferably alone, but felt he should have something significant to offer, at least, say, a place on the board. Steve would need no reminder that charitable gifts have tax advantages. "But," James asked, "how about putting his name, or his mother's, on the new center?" James argued that Steve was not only wealthy but had connections to wealth, just what the board and HOPE needed. In fact, Steve would make a good campaign chair! He would be flattered to be asked, could use some good publicity, and of course was grateful for the care HOPE gave his dying mother. James conceded that the board had no policy for naming buildings, but felt members would support him if the gift represented at least half of the center's cost. Besides, he reminded the committee, Steve might be their best—and likely only—bet for leadership to make the campaign goal.

If some committee members were uneasy about Stephen's reputation or the origins of his wealth, they did not say so; the prospect of that kind of money was unprecedented in HOPE's history. The committee agreed: Invite him to be a member of the board (surely the current members will go along). Ask him for a leadership gift (he could at least be "honorary chair" if he helped solicit other gifts), and note that a gift of $250,000 or more would name the center.

Although a majority of the board concurred, some abstained. James subsequently recruited Steve, and received what James later reported was the "promise of a large gift," as yet undetermined, pending the outcome of certain complex financial arrangements Steve would have to make—with James's help.

Commentary

The handling of research here is suspect for showing lack of respect (privacy, confidentiality) to a possible donor. Cheryl gathered the information, though public, dishonestly (contrary to the principle of trust) to avoid detection, then stored it along with intimate anecdotes in files accessible to other staff. To secure Stephen's gift, the lawyer, James, offered non-charitable inducements, to the jeopardy of beneficence; and the board committee assumed a precarious posture by associating HOPE with questionable wealth and reputation at the possible expense of public trust. James's personal and professional relationship with Steve may also subject HOPE to various conflicts of interest in the future and possibly serve to compensate James for services required by Steve's financial affairs. How might one have resolved this situation more appropriately and ethically?

Clearly, one may continue to imagine other episodes of ethical ambiguity in this and other cases. Indeed, raising "what if" questions is an excellent way to develop one's ethical agility.

However, perhaps we should not conclude with the trials and ethical tensions of the HOPE organization before noting that of course there are some outstanding models of nonprofit activity in the nation that are worthy of study and emulation.[3] For example, based on extensive studies of organizational effectiveness that includes board responsibility for legal compliance and ethical conduct, leaders of voluntary organizations and community foundations have identified ten nonprofit groups for their overall excellence. They have four distinguishing marks in common: (1) a clear sense of mission by which the board and staff consistently guide themselves; (2) a leader who creates a culture that enables and motivates the organization to fulfill its mission; (3) an involved and committed volunteer board that provides a bridge to the larger community; and (4) an ongoing capacity to attract the financial and human resources sufficient to support the organization's program.

Whether these outstanding organizations also have codes of ethics by which they regularly evaluate their decision-making is not known. This need, of vital importance to every nonprofit, is addressed in the following and final chapter.

Five   A Practitioner's Code of Ethics

When Aristotle talks about responsibility he makes a distinction between our professional, social, or cultural role, and our moral obligation. It is quite possible to play the role of fundraiser, grant-maker, or nonprofit volunteer well, and yet fail to think and act in an ethically responsible way. The ultimate aim is to consistently fuse these responsibilities together.

The distinction is particularly important for understanding codes of ethics, where the two kinds of responsibility meet. No doubt Aristotle would affirm the need and usefulness of codes for business, government, and the professions as we know them today. With the almost daily allegations of influence-peddling, cover-ups, and deception of Congress under oath, not to mention white collar fraud, conflicts of interest, and intrusion into privacy, there is good reason to have effective codes of conduct in public, private, and nonprofit sectors of society.[1] Like a vast network of limited social contracts, these codes are both implicit and explicit. They are central to the pluralistic, patchwork fabric of personal and organizational commitments that uniquely hold contemporary American society together.

CODES AND CONFLICTS OF INTEREST

In a narrow sense, the process of developing a code characterizes ethics itself, seen by some as the locus for conflict of values. The provisions of a code are general resolutions of potential areas of tension and conflict that are part of the organization's environment.

For this reason, codes typically give special attention to actual and potential conflicts of interest, which can be very subtle. In fact, former President Bush once made the development of a new code governing the conduct of public servants a national priority, and declared that "apparent" conflict of interest, a concern basic to government service as well as corporate behavior, should be its guiding principle. That is, a government servant should avoid any action that has even the *appearance* of being at odds with public or corporate policy.

However, to define ethics solely in terms of conflict of interest is too simplistic. It makes some people content with the "smell test"—the presumption that we are all equipped with the capacity to sense when something is not right. We can just feel it.

Ironically, the concern for apparently conflicting interests can itself be abused, turning as it does upon intentions. To note that a particular relationship poses an apparent conflict can be a positive, well-intended request to erase suspicion, or it may be a mischievous charge intended solely to create suspicion. "Full disclosure" of the party's personal, business, or political interests is a common antidote. But at best, disclosure functions as a preventive measure in advance of possible conflict. It does little to resolve a conflict ethically in a framework for decision-making. Like the code itself, an apparent conflict of interest is basically an invitation to *do* ethics.

A related and intriguing test is offered by Harlan Cleveland in *The Future Executive*.[2] "If this action is held up to public scrutiny, will I still feel that it is what I should have done, and how I should have done it?" A colloquial version of this principle was offered recently by a major nonprofit director, who urged nonprofits to draft policy that considers how it will play "on a 20-second news bite or in a four-inch newspaper column."

Cleveland's principle assumes that our intentions will be found out. "Information leaks," so we might as well reveal it in the best possible light. However, we may recall Plato's legend of the Ring of Gyges, described in his *Republic*.[3] Suppose, according to the legend—a test of moral intentions in its own right—one had a magic ring enabling a person to become invisible, allowing one to do anything one pleased with impunity. Would there be any reason to refrain from unqualified self-interest? Actually there is, argues Socrates (Plato's dramatic agent). Even if we had this ring—and occasionally we think we do—it would be self-destructive to use it, harmful to the "soul," the seat of character, the basis for well-being.

Without careful qualification, Cleveland's test is a mixed blessing. Public scrutiny of policy affairs generally assures openness, a cornerstone of American democracy, but the weight of public opinion in no way assures rightness. As a test of consistency with implicit or explicit public policy, it may be fine. As a principle of *ethical adequacy*, it borders closely on the principle of expediency, or, as the cynical saying goes, whatever is "politically correct."

By themselves codes offer little improvement, but they do have two important public benefits. In the first place, they guide us to identify, objectify, and verbally safeguard important interests or values of the individual, the organization, and others including the public at large—every person who has a stake in our purposes.

A second benefit is a code's potential for eliciting trust. Neither the individual nor the public at large can have complete confidence in an organization whose norms run aground on the Scylla and Charybdis of inconsistency and hypocrisy. The code is a public witness that the organization recognizes and seeks to honor the value of trust in its relationships.

Thus, a code of ethics can be a powerful organizational instrument. Even so, if Aristotle is right about the importance of differentiating professional and moral responsibilities, there is a certain mischievous seduction about having a code.

THE PROBLEM WITH CODES

Codes have the look, but not the weight of moral principle. Unless they are supported by what it means to think and act in an ethically responsible manner (chapter 2), codes tempt one to substitute their normative provisions for the ethical character and principles that justify them. As a set of commitments or values shared by a group with a common purpose, a code represents the normative role we as professionals or volunteers are willing to assume in our relationships with all who are perceived to have a stake in the organization. A code is specifically written to reflect the organization's mission, and its moral intentions. However, by its very nature a code has two major shortcomings: first, as a standard of ethical conduct, it is *not self-justifying*; and second, as a guide to practical action, it is *not self-clarifying*.

For example, we do not assume that because the Mafia has a code, its norms are ethically self-evident. Despite their moral ring, norms proposing "honor among thieves," or absolute loyalty to "the company," or "my country right or wrong," are not necessarily justified. That will not happen until they are derived from more fundamental, generally durable and widely acknowledged principles of conduct, such as truth-telling, promise-keeping, respect for persons, and the like.

A recent study of white-collar crime, principally fraud, reveals how the unethical mind works.[4] Ranging from employees who pad their expense accounts to those who steal money by altering an organization's records, the fraudulently disposed are represented at every level of responsibility. Typically tempted by the prospect of enriching themselves with impunity at the expense of the organization, then moved by greed, they seize the opportunity. If found out and questioned about their dishonesty, according to one convicted executive, most deny their culpability with "a million excuses, ranging from, 'I did it to keep the business afloat' to, 'Hey, I'm not some violent criminal. I didn't hurt anybody.' " In fact, some try to justify it as only right and fair considering that their real value to the organization goes unrecognized! However, the executive insists, "[white collar criminals are the worst in the world] because they use their intelligence, education, status and trust [that others have in them] for their own benefit." The study also finds that the most frequently cited step (79 percent) that companies may take to reduce the possibility of fraud—an increasingly substantial expense—is to establish a corporate code of conduct.

Nonetheless, content with a few normative provisions, we expect too much of a code. Without the ethical awareness and reasoning that clarify and justify its norms, a code has little power despite our best intentions to effect right action.

HABITS OF AN ETHICAL ORGANIZATION

Code provisions are only generalizations, static but open-ended guides for organizing the dynamic and often complex day-to-day experiences that demand specific, moral actions. A code's provisions are not self-clarifying, short of the concrete situations that make them meaningful.

National organizations such as the Council for the Advancement and Support of Education (CASE) have long had codes governing their members. In fundraising alone, the profession has become so complex and technical as to warrant specialized codes for areas such as planned giving, prospect research, telemarketing and direct mail, as well as volunteer and board development. The codes of national organizations make excellent models of the standards common to the professions. However, they are no substitute for codes specifically developed in each organization. Indeed, a footnote to the CASE code says it is "intended to stimulate ethical awareness and discussion."[5]

A code that is skeined but never woven strategically into the fabric of day-to-day experience is purely sentimental, a cedar chest item. Printed and distributed merely to elicit good will, it borders on moralistic promotionalism. Unless the organization regularly reviews its standards in the light of experience, developing a code can be a substantial waste of time and talent, and a potential object of cynicism for those who have a stake in it.

Ideally, a code is programmatic, begging to be examined in the course of carrying out the organization's multiple objectives. Its utility and meaningfulness are embodied by example, by the cases we encounter in the trenches. As Michael O'Neill, director of the Institute for Nonprofit Organization Management, has put it, ethics is the business of nonprofits. It should be examined broadly and regularly by practitioners, not only when the occasional crisis arises.[6]

Thus, regular occasion to discuss current strategies with reference to the code serves to heighten ethical issues, exemplify the code's norms, and test them—together with organizational plans—for adequacy. There is no substitute for developing a code that is tempered by local fires.

ETHICAL LEADERSHIP

A code is only as effective as the corporate will and leadership behind it. The topic of ethics and leadership has been covered amply by other authors,[7] though we noted at the outset that Aristotle's *Nichomachean Ethics* may well set the ideal example for the philanthropic community. Indeed, we could make the case that the essence of leadership, at least in philanthropy if not elsewhere, *is* to be ethical. Or perhaps better stated: leaders are not by definition morally virtuous, but they ought to be.

A study once sought to define the connection between character development and leadership by noting what leaders conspicuous by their efforts to address human needs have in common.[8] The researcher found that such leaders are all competent, are committed to a worthy and transcendent mission, have a positive impact on their organization and community, care about human beings, and have the integrity, perseverance, and courage to stand up for their convictions (at times to their own jeopardy). But they can also laugh at themselves.

For every practitioner of philanthropy, there is a profound lesson in this: we cannot all assume conspicuous leadership positions, but we can all be ethical leaders in the roles we do assume. We can be models of character, whenever integrity and courage to do the right thing are at stake. Achieving corporate responsibility will be difficult if not impossible without strong leadership at the top. Ethical leadership cannot effectively be delegated or left to consultants.

THE ELEMENTS OF A CODE

Every code is unique, tailored to the organization's aims and stakeholders. However, codes also tend to have elements in common. Typically, they:

- o begin with a statement of *purpose* that implies or affirms a service for the public good;
- o identify major *stakeholders*, and the responsibilities that are assumed in relation to each;
- o affirm good *citizenship*, upholding both the letter and the spirit of state and federal laws;
- o proclaim a commitment to *ethical principles* that exceed compliance with the law ("obedience to the unenforceable");

- promulgate a *governing ethical concept*, a dominant theme or relationship such as trust, that is central to the organization's nature;
- identify—where necessary—*private and public interests* consistent with the organization's accountability and the acknowledged democratic rights of all; and,
- give special attention to the principal *conflicts of interest* that can arise in pursuit of objectives.

ABOUT CORPORATE RESPONSIBILITY

There are three common views of corporate responsibility, from which every organization can learn. They tend to define the ethical culture.

First, there is the view, consistent with classical capitalism, that a corporation's primary duty is to generate profit, without which jobs, family security, and taxes cannot be sustained. Corporations that compete fairly and openly, managed in the best interests of the *shareholder*, economically benefit society. For the nonprofit cause this means above all satisfying the donor's expectations that contributions are used efficiently and effectively to further the organization's mission.

The second view, the *stakeholder* concept, recognizes a broader accountability to society. In addition to serving their owners, corporations have responsibilities to everyone who has a stake in the business, including the community. Indeed, as firms aid in solving the community's social problems, they not only help society prosper but are likely to themselves be more profitable. Similarly, the nonprofit finds it in its own best interests to be attentive to a constituency larger than its donors and the targeted recipients of its funds; the whole community has a stake in the organization's efforts.

Third, there is the view that society is best served when corporations—and nonprofits—are *regulated*, by the government or some authoritative body, to conform to the highest possible standards of personal and community life. Left to its own self-interests, a corporation or organization may well make up its own rules as it goes along, to the detriment of the greater good. Thus, a state's charities agency may set a limit on how much of a nonprofit's funds raised should be spent on raising them.

Most corporate bodies tend to favor the stakeholder view, and hold that self-regulation, wherever it is effective, is better than government intervention. However, a corporation's social responsibility, often reflected in its code, is a separate and major topic, worthy of its own forum and outside the limits of this book. For example, a strong case can be made for a corporation that, while actively committed to socially worthy causes, sees its first responsibility to the shareholder. That view has been demonstrated compellingly in recent cases where the well-promoted programs of corporations to serve a popular public good entailed short-sighted management strategies that resulted in significant layoffs and loss of benefits to long-time employees, substantial losses to shareholders (many of whom were employees), and a diminished corporate image.[9]

Among outstanding examples of corporate stakeholder codes of ethics are those of American Can Company, Johnson & Johnson, and Levi Strauss & Co.[10] For example, in its opening section, "Our Shared Responsibilities," American Can makes the commitment to serve its stakeholders—customers, suppliers, shareholders, employees, and community—by noting (with Aristotle) that it is not enough to meet performance goals. Employment at American Can also requires a clear understanding and embodiment of the company's ethical standards. The basic rules are: to obey all laws applying to the business; to go beyond the letter of the law to its spirit, based on experience and conscience; and to let rules of fairness and honor govern one's conduct at all times. The code then develops the theme of accountability—in business relationships, to employees, to society, and to the law—with helpful examples of acceptable and unacceptable conduct. Moreover, the code is intended "to create a continuing dialogue producing thoughtful and positive action, characterized by mutual respect and understanding." It is an excellent statement of a corporation's responsibilities to its various stakeholders.

Of similar quality, and often held up as a model for corporate conduct, the succinct Johnson & Johnson code or "credo" stands out for placing its customers and the community before its shareholders. It begins: "WE believe our first responsibility is to the doctors, nurses and patients, to mothers and all others who use our products and services." A few brief provisions later: "WE are responsible to our employees, the men and women who work with us throughout the world. EVERYONE must be considered as an individual. WE must respect their dignity and recognize their merit." The final section begins, "OUR final responsibility is to our stockholders. BUSINESS must make a sound profit." The code is also noteworthy for undergoing intense review on a regular basis, to insure that it is a living document, embraced by all employees, including management. While these company-wide discussions have led some over the years to resist the credo's character, the company has continued to affirm the principles virtually without change since 1975. The firm's handling of the famous Tylenol tragedy, when it took millions of dollars worth of the product off the shelves to develop a tamper-proof container and stop any further attempts by culprits to lace it with cyanide, is legendary. It demonstrated the integrity of the company and the efficacy of its code. Among the results, though presumably not the governing motives, were heightened good will and profitability.

Like Johnson & Johnson, Levi Strauss & Co. has consistently demonstrated its commitment to a code of ethical principles, notable for the provision on integrity: "We will live up to LS&CO's ethical principles; even when confronted by personal, professional and social risks, as well as economic pressures." The code also provides its own governing principle, suggesting that "the best test whether something is ethically correct is whether you would be prepared to present it to our senior management and board of directors as being consistent with our ethical traditions: If you have any uneasiness about an action you are about to take or which you see, you should discuss the action with your supervisor or management."

The code of ethics developed by Stanford University's Office of Development is one of the oldest and finest examples for nonprofit fundraisers in education.[11] Again, more a "credo" than a comprehensive code of ethical principles, it effectively sets forth the office's "mission and values" in seven succinct paragraphs covering: a mission that recognizes dual accountability, to donors as well as to the institution; a responsibility for donor privacy and gift confidentiality; integrity; teamwork; quality; enthusiasm (to be effective, one must be positive!); and initiative. The paragraph on integrity, the dominant ethical theme, is an eloquent series of practitioner commitments:

> We live up to both the spirit and letter of promises to donors. As staff members, we avoid conflicts of interest between our Stanford jobs and outside activities, both paid and voluntary. We do not exploit relationships with donors or volunteers for personal benefit. We utilize University facilities and property only for official business. We travel with a sense of fiscal responsibility. When in doubt about the compatibility of an action or expenditure with these values, we have a responsibility to disclose and discuss the situation with relevant [Office of Development] managers.

A GUIDE TO CODE DEVELOPMENT

A guide, designed mainly for an organization's development operations, may be helpful. It may be viewed as a modest complement and follow-up to the principles, examples, and "key ethical questions" found in the Independent Sector (IS) study and follow-up workbook.[12] In the best traditions of American philanthropy, they provide a rationale, a set of values, and a self-study instrument to encourage ethical behavior in all nonprofit organizations. However, their purpose falls short of providing the practitioner with a comprehensive program—the aim of this book—for more fully understanding ethical awareness and decision-making. Code or no code, one's stated values, including a code's provisions, will be most effective when regularly clarified by experience and supported by principle.

Nonetheless, the essential values or behaviors the IS committee believes should be common to all independent sector organizations are eminently worthy of being reflected in a nonprofit's code, and consistent with what follows. For convenience they are repeated here:

o commitment beyond self
o commitment beyond the law
o commitment to the public good
o respect for the value and dignity of individuals
o tolerance, diversity and social justice
o accountability to the public
o openness and honesty
o prudent application of resources
o obedience to the laws

The IS companion workbook asks a number of key questions for self-evaluation by the nonprofit under each of these behavior categories. The workbook will serve the nonprofit well as a systematic means to "audit" its ethical dispositions both prior to the development of a code and afterwards on a regular basis to maintain the code's efficacy. Noteworthy among the workbook's key questions are these: "Are all persons associated with the organization educated in the meaning and importance of the code and ethical conduct?"; and, "Can I articulate the organization's mission and recognize my own role in achieving that mission?". What the workbook will not do (and was not intended to do) is to resolve the ethical tensions that the practitioner faces from day to day.

The model code offered below assumes that the nonprofit's basic mission and case statements have been reviewed. The headings and sample provisions are conceptual pieces only, intended for vigorous, ongoing discussion. They represent some basic elements that should be considered in a code, with room for others that may be needed to reflect the organization's unique culture.

The provisions reflect the three major ethical principles or dominant spheres of influence, and their supporting principles, discussed with examples in chapter 4:

RESPECT
Autonomy (self-determination)
Privacy
Protection (concern for others)

BENEFICENCE
> Serving the good
> Charitable intent

TRUST
> Truth-telling
> Promise-keeping
> Accountability (stewardship)
> Fairness
> Fidelity of purpose (consistency)

The organization may wish to present its guiding principles independently of the full code, developed around the language in chapter 4. Of course, the principles are themselves subject to each nonprofit's own discussions and sound—quite possibly better—ethical judgment.

Here are some provisions to consider in the development of a code for nonprofit practitioners of philanthropy:

Purpose

> As responsible persons organized to advance and support [the organization's mission], our primary objective is to aid [name of the organization] in accomplishing its purposes by rightly soliciting the contributions and enduring good will of our constituents.

Stakeholder Relationships

> In partnership with the philanthropic community, we will maintain our professional and ethical relationships with donors whose gifts are entrusted to us; with volunteers on whose aid we depend; with staff who are accountable for their actions; and with the public whose well-being we serve.

Responsible Citizenship

> As responsible citizens of this community and nation, we uphold both the letter and the spirit of the law, and all rights and privileges afforded by the law to every citizen.

Ethical Principles beyond the Law

> We also acknowledge the propriety and self-enforcement

of ethical principles and human rights that may exceed compliance with existing laws.

[Here, the organization may wish to add, with help from chapter 4, its list of principles or ethical values, including the primary principles and related ones such as autonomy, privacy, protection, serving the good, charitable intent, truthfulness, promise-keeping, accountability, fairness, fidelity of purpose, or others suggested in the provisions to follow.]

The remaining provisions focus on the organization's concerns and values. For example, every nonprofit development operation has a responsibility to protect the organization's nonprofit autonomy and the donor's privacy even as the public good is served. The key to striking this balance lies in clarifying the relationship between two kinds of trust—private and public—and the "need to know." The latter idea is, in principle, vague until the lines we draw specify and help to justify what we mean.

Based on the primary ethical principle of trust, and specifically on its derivative, promise-keeping, the donor/prospect must have confidence in the nonprofit to solicit, handle, and direct contributions properly and as advertised. By an ethical requirement that goes beyond law, these functions represent the organization's fiduciary duty, that is, what it holds in both public and private trust. Thus, a nonprofit might introduce this topic in the following way:

Public and Private Trust

In a pluralistic, democratic society the nonprofit organization exists in a variety of forms to serve the charitable, educational, and social good of all.

[For the typical development operation:] As an integral part of [the organization] and thus dedicated to support its purposes, we have a preeminent fiduciary responsibility to all who provide charitable gifts and services on our behalf.

[Or, the fundraising foundation:] Though the [name of the foundation] exists solely to support [the organization], it has a fiduciary responsibility to all who provide charitable gifts and services on its behalf.

The individual has the ethical and (in the case of public employees) legal right to personal privacy, grounded in the primary principle of *respect*. The organization accords the individual confidentiality, to safeguard this right against intrusiveness into gift records and intimately personal information, except when the individual consents to disclosure.

However, we are also committed to a *public* trust. Public disclosure of the organization's financial and other data safeguards the public and the organization against conflicts of interest and the abuse and misuse of policies and funds. Arm's-length audits of the sources and uses of funds avoid mischievous allegations that, for example, "slush funds" exist for surreptitious purposes. A policy for proper disclosure is also a preventive measure: its absence may encourage unnecessary intrusiveness of another kind, namely, governmental regulation.

Thus, the following provisions may serve to take these factors into account:

As an American institution, [the organization] values autonomy sufficient to safeguard a proper division of organizational, private, and public interests. Thus, we recognize a dual responsibility for the trust in which both public and private interests hold us; that is:

We disclose all financial statements, governing policies, and plans of action that add to public understanding, appreciation and confidence in our objectives. However, we are equally concerned to guard against unwarranted interference and intrusiveness into private matters, particularly confidential information, such as a donor's gift history or personal life.

These provisions lead directly into the next section of the code, covering the organization's position on fundraising, based on the primary principle of *beneficence*. For example:

Fundraising

As [the organization] seeks to raise funds, it joins with private individuals, firms, foundations, and the public at large to [statement of mission], which benefits the community and therefore is worthy of its support.
To that end, we are scrupulous in our efforts to accomplish our donors' purposes, to prudently manage all funds, and to di-

rect discretionary gifts to objectives that are open to public scrutiny.

The last provisions focus on the responsibilities of fundraising staff and on volunteer commitment. As noted in chapter 3, increasing sophistication in the gathering and management of donor/prospect information makes it more important than ever to be up front about the care one takes to assure donor confidentiality, consent to disclosure, and enduring trust.

Thus:

Information Management

Whether represented by volunteers or professional staff, [the organization] seeks to assure its own integrity and that of others in the use and management of information.

We are thorough and discreet in the process of learning to know and engage all donors and prospective supporters, to earn their enduring support.

We do this with sensitivity and respect for individual and corporate dignity; and we hold confidential, save with the person's or organization's consent to disclose it, private or corporate information such as gift transactions, personal identity, and anecdotal knowledge, whether on or off the record.

Next, the conflict of interest provisions of the code will underscore again the importance of trust as the fundraiser's *modus operandi*, and may even specify the unethical character of conflicting or competing interests. In addition, as noted in the case material in chapter 3, given the rightful, but also extremely vulnerable position of the "whistle-blower" in organizational activity, the section should offer a provision to anticipate such cases.

Conflict of Interest

As persons employed or enlisted for our willingness, competence, and effectiveness in philanthropy, we are committed to integrity in all our relationships, and place the long-term best interests of [the organization], its constituents, and the profession before our own.

To avoid even the appearance of conflicting or competing interests, we make no agreements that could result in favoritism, unfair advantage, or monetarily significant reward for ourselves or [the organization].

Concerns about any transaction or relationship that could embarrass [the organization], breach confidentiality, or violate conscience will be discussed with those to whom we are accountable, fairly and without fear of recrimination.

The final provisions of the code are the most personal of all. They affirm the individual staff member's or volunteer's readiness—as the classical ethicists enjoin—to embody character that is worthy of philanthropy. As I have stressed throughout the book, individual as well as organizational character are the wellsprings of ethical thought and action, whatever the governing framework for their justification. Particularly in the nonprofit sector, character is the personal and corporate good will behind the respect, beneficence, and trust we seek to develop.

This provision of the code should include a practitioner's conduct in the profession at large as well as in his/her own organization. Disrespect for the work of others, misrepresenting personal expense accounts, careless use of the organization's property, negligent security, and indifference to the need for professional improvement all exemplify inappropriate behavior that we may wish to cite specifically. The provision serves as a personal credo for staff and board members and other volunteers who work for the organization.

Personal Character

As individuals we are ethically responsible to ourselves and our profession for embodying character that is worthy of the best traditions of philanthropy. To that end we will compromise neither our personal convictions nor those of the organization and its constituents.

As professionals we treat our colleagues here and elsewhere with respect and properly credit others for ideas not our own. We use budgeted funds prudently, and account for them honestly. We are careful with facilities and equipment, and safeguard the integrity of records and systems to which we have access. And, we acknowledge the value of constructive criticism, to evaluate and improve our performance against the profession's highest standards.

As the examples of effectively ethical organizations suggest, a code may be shorter and more succinct, or more extensive and explicit, than the model above. What is important is that it be tailored to the organization's character and environment, and that it express the essential norms that define one's practice of philanthropy.

Above all, this book has urged, practitioners must learn how to think and act in an ethically responsible way, how to make principled decisions, and how to consistently embody and regularly examine their own organizational code of ethics.

THE CASE FOR DOING THE RIGHT THING

No one said that being ethical would be easy, least of all Aristotle. To him, it means to take responsibility, be accountable for our actions. Why should we? Because, as reason and experience teach us, there are limits beyond which it is unwise for human beings to go. If so, we must learn how and where to draw the line. What is more, by doing so we begin to build admirable, virtuous character, realize our potential, and experience the kind of well-being in life we all seek.

To Aristotle, taking responsibility for one's actions means not only being self-conscious agents and skillful role-players who do things right. It also means doing the right thing, above all in matters of justice and beneficence, the realm of morality. However, as he observed, doing the right thing has never been as predictable as following the rules of geometry. Deciding where to draw the line—the Golden Mean—between action that goes too far or not far enough is an art one develops with experience. Indeed, beneficence demands two artful, right-seeking actions: gaining wealth and distributing it. And, since one's governing motive is to enhance the public good, charitable intent is fundamental to ethical philanthropy.

Aristotle's view of philanthropy is the classical ideal. Still, the long-standing tradition of sharing one's resources with those who are without them—the alternative idealized by Jesus—is clearly more popular today in both its religious and secular forms. For over a million nonprofits in this country, philanthropy—understood as volunteer action for the common good—is efficacious and vital.

Ethical responsibility—or accountability—is both an individual and a corporate matter. The intersection of agency, role-playing, and action is corporately expressed by its culture and ideally by its code of ethical values and behaviors. The responsible firm or nonprofit embodies its code, committing its members both to keep the law of the land and to exceed it by employing the organization's moral norms. However, a code is impotent unless its practitioners know how to think and act in an ethically responsible way; that is, how to focus, frame, and justify their actions.

Ethics is basically a matter of principle. Both Aristotle and Jesus offer broadly governing principles such as the Golden Mean and the Golden Rule. But neither is adequate without qualification. Aristotle's Mean is so general as to leave completely relative what is right for each person in each situation. And Jesus' Rule, secularly applied, is ambiguously self-interested unless one provides a carefully developed notion of self-respect.

The first challenge in doing the right thing is to avoid expediency and radical individualism—to find principles governing action that are if possible always right for most if not all people. Knowing right from wrong does not begin in a vacuum. We regularly make moral judgments and opinions based on personal experience and values. Some look to conscience developed from childhood, or to rules and traditions reinforced by laws. Others say common sense requires simple respect for others, and many seem to believe that one is free to do as one pleases, as long as it does no harm.

Indeed, we often give such judgments and opinions obligatory force, with an ought or a should. But no moral opinion is better or more obligatory than any other in the absence of criteria by which to judge them. Thinking ethically, not merely being opinionated or comfortable with what is culturally permissible, is about clarifying and resolving differences, conflicting attitudes, competing tensions between what we claim or judge to be right and wrong. But it is also about doing it, not merely saying it.

In short, we need an ethical framework that is adequate for relieving the tensions involved in doing the right thing. Ethical adequacy requires:

1. *Clarity of thinking.* We must know the facts, understand one another, be open and reasonable if we hope to get at the ethical issue we must address.

2. *Self-examination.* We must honestly confront the human condition and its capacity for good and evil, because the efficacy of moral action depends on what we as human beings can truly accomplish.

3. *Acknowledgment that ethical relationships are based on trust.* In matters of philanthropy, trust is the moral culture in which we operate.

4. *Durable principles.* We need these to consistently clarify moral ambiguities and ward off hypocrisy, which we find intolerable.

5. *Moral judgments that are justifiable.* These are achieved by conformity to principles we commonly respect and ultimately by a governing outlook that grounds and guides all our action.

From a secular standpoint, two classical frameworks exemplify these conditions: the utilitarian framework inspired by Mill, and the duty-based framework developed by Kant. For the utilitarian—or consequentialist—view, an act is ethically worthy when its consequences or effects are more beneficial than harmful for most people, most of the time. Truth-telling, for example, is ethically worthy for that reason. For the duty-based—or imperativist—view, an act is ethically worthy, independent of consequences, when done for the sake of duty, as determined by what is universally appropriate and consistent with reason. Truth-telling is such a duty.

Although as competing views they are popularly simplified as beneficial consequences versus good intentions, both the classic frameworks and the moral tensions they address are more complex. While these frameworks seem inadequate to resolve all of life's dilemmas, either is generally adequate to ground principled action for practitioners, and may be adopted.

Even with good moral instincts, one develops the art of detecting moral tensions mainly from experience with cases typical of the profession, that is: (1) those affecting donors or prospects, such as misusing donor funds and information, intruding on donor privacy, exploiting donors to one's advantage, etc.; and (2) those affecting the organization, like compromising its interests, misusing property, charging inappropriately for services, mistreating the whistle-blower, etc. To address these cases and issues we generally require two kinds of decision-making: (a) drawing lines, often related to potential abuse; and (b) choosing between competing or conflicting courses of action both of which seem right.

However, we cannot do the right thing without knowing which action is right and how to justify it. To that end we need at least two, and ideally three additional instruments:

1. *A set of ethical principles.* The principles of greatest influence in philanthropy are respect, beneficence, and trust. They, in turn, imply principles such as confidentiality, service, accountability, fairness, truth-telling, fidelity, etc.

2. *A decision-making procedure.* Certain questions should be asked as a matter of routine: What seems right or wrong about this situation? What course of action seems best? What principles (and governing framework) would justify the action?

The ideal framework for principled action would include 3. *A code of ethics.* We need a public set of shared values and behaviors regularly clarified and justified by the experience of those who have a stake in the organization. Tailored to the mission and environment of the nonprofit's philanthropic work, the code will include explicit ethical positions relating to purpose, stakeholders, citizenship, ethical principles, public trust, fundraising, information, conflict of interest, and personal character.

In matters of philanthropy and everywhere, being accountable to ourselves and others means taking ethically principled action: doing the right thing.

Appendix

Selected Ethical Codes, Principles, and Standards

PHILANTHROPY is based on voluntary action for the common good. It is a tradition of giving and sharing that is primary to the quality of life. To assure that philanthropy merits the respect and trust of the general public, and that donors and prospective donors can have full confidence in the not-for-profit organizations and causes they are asked to support, we declare that all donors have these rights:

I. To be informed of the organization's mission, of the way the organization intends to use donated resources, and of its capacity to use donations effectively for their intended purposes.

II. To be informed of the identity of those serving on the organization's governing board, and to expect the board to exercise prudent judgment in its stewardship responsibilities.

III. To have access to the organization's most recent financial statements.

IV. To be assured their gifts will be used for the purposes for which they were given.

V. To receive appropriate acknowledgment and recognition.

VI. To be assured that information about their donations is handled with respect and with confidentiality to the extent provided by law.

VII. To expect that all relationships with individuals representing organizations of interest to the donor will be professional in nature.

VIII. To be informed whether those seeking donations are volunteers, employees of the organization, or hired solicitors.

IX. To have the opportunity for their names to be deleted from mailing lists that an organization may intend to share.

X. To feel free to ask questions when making a donation and to receive prompt, truthful, and forthright answers.

Developed by American Association of Fund Raising Counsel, Association for Healthcare Philanthropy, Council for Advancement and Support of Education, National Society of Fund Raising Executives; endorsed by (in formation) Independent Sector, National Catholic Development Conference, National Committee on Planned Giving, National Council for Resource Development, United Way of America.

NATIONAL SOCIETY OF FUND RAISING EXECUTIVES
Codes of Ethical Principles and Standards of Professional Practice

Statements of Ethical Principles
Adopted November 1991

The National Society of Fund Raising Executives exists to foster the development and growth of fund-raising professionals and the profession, to preserve and enhance philanthropy and volunteerism, and to promote high ethical standards in the fund-raising profession.

To these ends, this code declares the ethical values and standards of professional practice which NSFRE members embrace and which they strive to uphold in their responsibilities for generating philanthropic support.

Members of the National Society of Fund Raising Executives are motivated by an inner drive to improve the quality of life through the causes they serve. They seek to inspire others through their own sense of dedication and high purpose. They are committed to the improvements of their professional knowledge and skills in order that their performance will better serve others. They recognize their stewardship responsibility to ensure that needed resources are vigorously and ethically sought and that the intent of the donor is honestly fulfilled. Such individuals practice their profession with integrity, honesty, truthfulness and adherence to the absolute obligation to safeguard the public trust.

Furthermore, NSFRE members
o serve the ideal of philanthropy, are committed to the preservation and enhancement of volunteerism, and hold steward-

ship of these concepts as the overriding principle of professional life;

o put charitable mission above personal gain, accepting compensation by salary or set fee only;

o foster cultural diversity and pluralistic values and treat all people with dignity and respect;

o affirm, through personal giving, a commitment to philanthropy and its role in society;

o adhere to the spirit as well as the letter of all applicable laws and regulations;

o bring credit to the fund-raising profession by their public demeanor;

o recognize their individual boundaries of competence and are forthcoming about their professional qualifications and credentials;

o value the privacy, freedom of choice, and interests of all those affected by their actions;

o disclose all relationships which might constitute, or appear to constitute, conflicts of interest;

o actively encourage all their colleagues to embrace and practice these ethical principles;

o adhere to the following standards of professional practice in their responsibilities for generating philanthropic support.

STANDARDS OF PROFESSIONAL PRACTICE
ADOPTED AND INCORPORATED INTO THE NSFRE
CODE OF ETHICAL PRINCIPLES NOVEMBER 1992

1.   Members shall act according to the highest standards and visions of their institution, profession, and conscience.

2.   Members shall comply with all applicable local, state, provincial, and federal, civil, and criminal laws. Members should avoid the appearance of any criminal offense or professional misconduct.

3.   Members shall be responsible for advocating, within their own organizations, adherence to all applicable laws and regulations.

4. Members shall work for a salary or fee, not percentage-based compensation or a commission.

5. Members may accept performance-based compensation, such as bonuses, provided that such bonuses are in accord with prevailing practices within the members' own organizations and are not based on a percentage of philanthropic funds raised.

6. Members shall neither seek or accept finder's fees and shall, to the best of their ability, discourage their organizations from paying such fees.

7. Members shall disclose all conflicts of interest; such disclosure does not preclude or imply ethical impropriety.

8. Members shall accurately state their professional experience, qualifications, and expertise.

9. Members shall adhere to the principle that all donor and prospect information created by, or on behalf of, an institution is the property of that institution and shall not be transferred or removed.

10. Members shall, on a scheduled basis, give donors the opportunity to have their names removed from lists which are sold to, rented to, or exchanged with other organizations.

11. Members shall not disclose privileged information to unauthorized parties.

12. Members shall keep constituent information confidential.

13. Members shall take care to ensure that all solicitation materials are accurate and correctly reflect the organization's mission and use of solicited funds.

14. Members shall, to the best of their ability, ensure that contributions are used in accordance with donors' intentions.

15. Members shall ensure, to the best of their ability, proper stewardship of charitable contributions, including: careful investment of funds; timely reports on the use and management of funds; and explicit consent by the donor before altering the conditions of a gift.

16. Members shall ensure, to the best of their ability, that donors receive informed and ethical advice about the value and tax implications of potential gifts.

Reprinted by permission of the National Society of Fund Raising Executives.

ASSOCIATION FOR HEALTHCARE PHILANTHROPY
STATEMENT OF PROFESSIONAL
STANDARDS AND CONDUCT
PREAMBLE

Association for Healthcare Philanthropy members represent to the public, by personal example and conduct, both their employer and their profession. They have, therefore, a duty to faithfully adhere to the highest standards and conduct in:

I. Their promotion of the merits of their institutions and of excellence in health care generally, providing community leadership in cooperation with health, educational, cultural, and other organizations;

II. Their words and actions, embodying respect for truth, honesty, fairness, free inquiry, and the opinions of others, treating all with equality and dignity;

III. Their respect for all individuals without regard to race, color, sex, creed, ethnic or national identity, handicap or age;

IV. Their commitment to strive to increase professional and personal skills for improved service to their donors and institutions, to encourage and actively participate in career development for themselves and others whose roles include support for resource development functions, and to share freely their knowledge and experience with others as appropriate;

V. Their continuing effort and energy to pursue new ideas and modifications to improve conditions for, and benefits to, donors and their institutions;

VI. Their avoidance of activities that might damage the reputation of any donor, their institution, any other resource development professional or the profession as a whole, or themselves, and to give full credit for the ideas, words, or images originated by others;

VII. Their respect for the rights of privacy of others and the confidentiality of information gained in the pursuit of their professional duties;

VIII. Their acceptance of a compensation method freely agreed upon and based on their institution's usual and customary compensation guidelines which have been established and approved for general institutional use while always remembering that: (a) any compensation agreement should fully reflect the standards of professional conduct; and, (b) antitrust laws in the United States prohibit limitation on compensation methods;

IX. Their respect for the law and professional ethics as a standard of personal conduct, with full adherence to the policies and procedures of their institution;

X. Their pledge to adhere to this statement of Professional Standards and Conduct, and to encourage others to join them in observance of its guidelines.

Reprinted by permission of the Association for Healthcare Philanthropy.

MODEL STANDARDS OF PRACTICE
FOR THE CHARITABLE GIFT PLANNER
PREAMBLE

The purpose of this statement is to encourage responsible charitable gift planning by urging the adoption of the following Standards of Practice by all who work in the charitable gift planning process, including charitable institutions and their gift planning officers, independent fund-raising consultants, attorneys, accountants, financial planners and life insurance agents, collectively referred to hereafter as "Gift Planners."

This statement recognizes that the solicitation, planning, and administration of a charitable gift is a complex process involving philanthropic, personal, financial, and tax considerations, and as such often involves professionals from various disciplines whose goals should include working together to structure a gift that achieves a fair and proper balance between the interests of the donor and the purposes of the charitable institution.

I. Primacy of Philanthropic Motivation

The principal basis for making a charitable gift should be a desire on the part of the donor to support the work of charitable institutions.

II. Explanation of Tax Implications

Congress has provided tax incentives for charitable giving, and the emphasis in this statement on philanthropic motivation in no way minimizes the necessity and appropriateness of a full and accurate explanation by the Gift Planner of those incentives and their implications.

III. Full Disclosure

It is essential to the gift planning process that the role and relationships of all parties involved, including how and by whom each is compensated, be fully disclosed to the donor. A Gift Planner shall not act or purport to act as a representative of any charity without the express knowledge and approval of the charity, and shall not be, while employed by the charity, act or purport to act as a representative of the donor, without the express consent of both the charity and the donor.

IV. Compensation

Compensation paid to Gift Planners shall be reasonable and proportionate to the services provided. Payments of finders fees, commissions or other fees by a donee organization to an independent Gift Planner as a condition for the delivery of a gift are never appropriate. Such payments lead to abusive practices and may violate certain state and federal regulations. Likewise, commission-based compensation for Gift Planners who are employed by a charitable institution is never appropriate.

V. Competence and Professionalism

The Gift Planner should strive to achieve and maintain a high degree of competence in his or her chosen area, and shall advise donors only in areas in which he or she is professionally qualified. It is the hallmark of professionalism for the Gift Planners that they realize when they have reached the limits of their knowledge and expertise, and as a result, should include other professionals in the process. Such relationships should be characterized by courtesy, tact and mutual respect.

VI. Consultations with Independent Advisors

A Gift Planner acting on behalf of a charity shall in all cases strongly encourage the donor to discuss the proposed gift with competent independent legal and tax advisors of the donor's choice.

VII. Consultation with Charities

Although Gift Planners frequently and properly counsel donors concerning specific charitable gifts without the prior knowledge or approval of the donee organization, the Gift Planner, in order to ensure that the gift will accomplish the donor's objectives, should encourage the donor, early in the gift planning process, to discuss the proposed gift with the charity to whom the gift is to be made. In cases where the donor desires anonymity, the Gift Planner shall endeavor, on behalf of the undisclosed donor, to obtain the charity's input in the gift planning process.

VIII. Explanation of Gift

The Gift Planner shall make every effort, insofar as possible, to insure that the donor receives a full and accurate explanation of all aspects of the proposed gift.

IX. Full Compliance

A Gift Planner shall fully comply with and shall encourage other parties in the gift planning process to fully comply with both the letter and the spirit of all applicable federal and state laws and regulations.

X. Public Trust

Gift Planners shall, in all dealings with donors, institutions, and other professionals, act with fairness, honesty, integrity, and openness. Except for compensation received for services, the terms of which have been disclosed to the donor, they shall have no vested interest that could result in personal gain.

Reprinted by permission of the National Committee on Planned Giving.

APRA MISSION STATEMENT

The *American Prospect Research Association* is a private nonprofit organization created to:

- o encourage professional development among members;
- o promote prospect research within nonprofit organizations;
- o act as a central source of professional information;
- o advance cooperative relationships; and
- o increase philanthropic resources of institutions served by members.

APRA Statement of Ethics

As representatives of the profession, American Prospect Research Association (APRA) members shall be respectful of all people and organizations. They shall support and further the individual's fundamental right to privacy. APRA members are committed to the ethical collection and use of information in the pursuit of legitimate institutional goals.

Code of Ethics

In their work, prospect researchers must balance the needs of their institutions/organizations to collect and record information with the prospects' right to privacy. This balance is not always easy to maintain. However, the following ethical principles apply:

I. Fundamental Principles
  A. Relevance
  Prospect Researchers shall seek and record only information that is relevant to the fund raising effort of the institutions that employ them.

B. Honesty

Prospect researchers shall be truthful with regard to their identity, purpose and the identity of their institution during the course of their work.

C. Confidentiality

Confidential information pertaining to donors or prospective donors shall be scrupulously protected so that the relationship of trust between donor and donee and the integrity of the prospect research professional is upheld.

D. Accuracy

Prospect researchers shall record all data accurately. Such information must be verifiable or attributable to its source.

II. Procedures

A. Collection

1. The collection and use of information shall be done lawfully.

2. Information sought and recorded may include all public records.

3. Written requests for public information shall be made on institutional stationery clearly identifying the sender.

4. Whenever possible, payments for public records shall be made through the institution.

5. When requesting information in person or by telephone, neither individual nor institutional identity shall be concealed.

B. Recording

1. Researchers shall state information in an objective and factual manner.

2. Documents pertaining to donors or prospective donors shall be irreversibly disposed of when no longer needed (e.g., by shredding).

C. Use

1. Non-public information is the property of the institution for which it was collected and shall not be given to persons other than those who are involved with the cultivation or solicitation effort or those who need that information in the performance of their duties for that institution.

2. Only public or published information may be shared with colleagues at other institutions as a professional courtesy.

3. Prospect information is the property of the institution for

which it was gathered and shall not be taken to another institution.

4. Prospect information shall be stored securely to prevent access by unauthorized persons.

5. Research documents containing donor or prospective donor information that are to be used outside research offices shall be clearly marked "confidential".

6. Special protection shall be afforded all giving records pertaining to anonymous donors.

Recommendations

1. Prospect researchers shall urge their institutions to develop written policies based upon the laws of their state defining what information shall be gathered and under what conditions it may be released and to whom.

2. Prospect researchers shall urge the development of written policies at their institutions defining who may authorize access to prospect files and under what conditions.

3. Prospect researchers shall urge their colleagues to abide by these principles of conduct.

Reprinted by permission of the American Prospect Research Association.

JOHNSON & JOHNSON
OUR CREDO

WE believe our first responsibility is to the doctors, nurses and patients, to mothers and all others who use our products and services.

IN meeting their needs everything we do must be of high quality.

WE must constantly strive to reduce our costs in order to maintain reasonable prices.

CUSTOMERS' orders must be serviced promptly and accurately.

OUR suppliers and distributors must have an opportunity to make a fair profit.

WE are responsible to our employees, the men and women who work with us throughout the world.

EVERYONE must be considered as an individual.

WE must respect their dignity and recognize their merit.

THEY must have a sense of security in their jobs.

COMPENSATION must be fair and adequate, and working conditions clean, orderly and safe.

EMPLOYEES must feel free to make suggestions and complaints.

THERE must be equal opportunity for employment, development and advancement for those qualified.

WE must provide competent management, and their actions must be just and ethical.

WE are responsible to the communities in which we live and work and to the world community as well.

WE must be good citizens—support good works and charities and bear our fair share of taxes.

WE must encourage civic improvements and better health and education.

WE must maintain in good order the property we are privileged to use, protecting the environment and natural resources.

OUR final responsibility is to our stockholders.

BUSINESS must make a sound profit.

WE must experiment with new ideas.

RESEARCH must be carried on, innovative programs developed and mistakes paid for.

NEW equipment must be purchased, new facilities provided and new products launched.

RESERVES must be created to provide for adverse times.

WHEN we operate according to these principles the stockholders should realize a fair return.

Reprinted by permission of Johnson & Johnson.

LEVI STRAUSS & CO.
ETHICAL PRINCIPLES

Our ethical principles are the values that set the ground rules for all that we do as employees of Levi Strauss & Co. As we seek to achieve responsible commercial success, we will be challenged to balance these principles against each other, always mindful of our promise to shareholders that we will achieve responsible commercial success.

The ethical principles are:

HONESTY: We will not say things that are false. We will never deliberately mislead. We will be as candid as possible, openly and freely sharing information, as appropriate to the relationship.

PROMISE-KEEPING: We will go to great lengths to keep our commitments. We will not make promises that can't be kept and we will not make promises on behalf of the company unless we have the authority to do so.

FAIRNESS: We will create and follow a process and achieve outcomes that a reasonable person would call just, even-handed and nonarbitrary.

RESPECT FOR OTHERS: We will be open and direct in our communication and receptive to influence. We will honor and value the abilities and contributions of others, embracing the responsibility and accountability for our actions in this regard.

COMPASSION: We will maintain an awareness of the needs of others and act to meet those needs whenever possible. We will also minimize harm whenever possible. We will act in ways that are consistent with our commitment to social responsibility.

INTEGRITY: We will live up to LS&CO's ethical principles; even when confronted by personal, professional and social risks, as well as economic pressures.

LEVI STRAUSS & CO.
CODE OF ETHICS

Levi Strauss & Co. has a long and distinguished history of ethical conduct and community involvement. Essentially, these are a reflection of the mutually shared values of the founding families and of our employees.

Our ethical values are based on the following elements:

o A commitment to commercial success in terms broader than merely financial measures.
o A respect for our employees, suppliers, customers, consumers and stockholders.

o A commitment to conduct which is not only legal but fair and morally correct in a fundamental sense.

o Avoidance of not only real, but the appearance of conflict of interest.

From time to time the Company will publish specific guidelines, policies and procedures. However, the best test whether something is ethically correct is whether you would be prepared to present it to our senior management and board of directors as being consistent with our ethical traditions. If you have any uneasiness about an action you are about to take or which you see, you should discuss the action with your supervisor or management.

Reprinted by permission of Levi Strauss & Co.

MISSION AND VALUES
STANFORD UNIVERSITY OFFICE OF DEVELOPMENT

Our Mission

Our collective and individual objective in the Office of Development is to support the mission of the University by maximizing, over the long term, useful gift support to Stanford, and doing so in ways that bring credit and benefit to the University, satisfaction to our donors, and fulfillment to our volunteers and staff. We underscore the importance of gift utility, acknowledging that funding priorities, which become our goals, are set by Stanford's senior academic administrators. Also, we avoid actions that would compromise the long term for the sake of short-term expediency. In addition, we recognize a dual responsibility to our donors as well as to the institution, and the pivotal role our volunteers play in making our mission possible.

Values Key to Our Mission

o *Responsibility to Donors*

We consider the donor's best financial interest, including capacity to give, taxes, cash flow, and estate planning. We disclose fully the conditions and status of any proposed or outstanding fund balance or pledge. Unless given permission by the donor, we regard gifts as confidential transactions between the donor and the University. We respect the privacy of donors and prospects, including requests for anonymity, and treat with great care any potentially sensitive information.

o Integrity

We live up to both the spirit and letter of promises to donors. As staff members, we avoid conflicts of interest between our Stanford jobs and outside activities, both paid and voluntary. We do not exploit relationships with donors or volunteers for personal benefit. We utilize University facilities and property only for official business. We travel with a sense of fiscal responsibility. When in doubt about the compatibility of an action or expenditure with these values, we have a responsibility to disclose and discuss the situation with relevant O[ffice] O[f] D[evelopment] managers.

o Teamwork

We recognize that success in our mission is always the result of team effort—staff teamwork, teamwork between staff and volunteers, and teamwork with other parts of the University. We pursue honest and open communication with volunteers, between supervisors and staff members, among peers and with officers, faculty, and staff throughout the University.

o Quality

Because for many of Stanford's friends, we are their primary contact with the University, we recognize our responsibility to reinforce the excellence of this University by the quality of our own work: our correspondence and communication, our personal interactions, the accuracy of our data, files, reports, and gift acknowledgments. Moreover, we believe that the pursuit of excellence is cost-efficient.

o *Enthusiasm*

We understand that unless we are supportive and positive about the mission of the University and our role in fulfilling that mission, we cannot be effective in our work. We understand that our public behavior must be guided by our dedication to the University.

o *Initiative*

We must initiate action and not simply respond to events and circumstances. We know that we must be willing to make our own decisions, take bold and independent action, and assume certain attendant personal (but not ethical) risks. When the best interests of the University are at stake, we are willing to undertake responsibilities beyond the normal scope of our jobs.
Henry E. Riggs
Vice President for Development

Reprinted by permission of Stanford University.

Notes

One   A QUESTION OF RESPONSIBILITY

Portions of this chapter are drawn from an earlier essay, "Aristotle and the Ethics of Philanthropy," *The Responsibilities of Wealth*, ed. Dwight Burlingame (Bloomington: Indiana University Press, 1992).

1. Aristotle, *The Nichomachean Ethics*, many versions; for example, J. A. K. Thomson's translation, *The Ethics of Aristotle* (New York: Penguin, 1956). The saying attributed to Aristotle is probably a paraphrase of his thoughts from Chaps. 1 and 2, Bk. IV; Bks. I, II, and III should also be read.

2. Among the best contemporary books on philanthropy is Robert L. Payton, *Philanthropy: Voluntary Action for the Public Good* (New York: American Council on Education, Macmillan, 1988); see especially the essays "Philanthropy as Moral Discourse" and "Virtue and Its Consequences." A comprehensive review of philanthropy as we know it in this country is Brian O'Connell's *Philanthropy in Action* (Washington, DC: Foundation Center, 1987). For a sense of the range of writings on philanthropy see Daphne Niobe Layton, *Philanthropy and Voluntarism* (Washington, DC: Foundation Center, 1987). Also, the Indiana University Center on Philanthropy, one of the nation's premier centers of philanthropic studies, houses the Payton Philanthropic Studies Library, the largest collection of books and dissertations on philanthropy in the nation. It also publishes *Philanthropic Studies Index*, a comprehensive guide to current periodical articles, books and other materials in the field.

3. Judith Babbits and Robert Dunn, "Being Ethical and Accountable in the Grantmaking Process," from *The Corporate Contributions Handbook: Devoting Private Means to Public Needs*, ed. James P. Shannon (San Francisco: Jossey-Bass, 1991), 332–40. This is a superb collection of essays by distinguished and experienced representatives of corporate philanthropy.

4. The definitive work on the I Ching is the translation by Richard Wilhelm (Princeton: Bollingen Series XIX, Princeton University Press, 1950).

5. See the Plato dialogues Euthyphro, Apology, Crito, many versions; for example the translation by F. J. Church (Indianapolis: Library of Liberal Arts, Bobbs-Merrill, 1956) for a good profile of Socrates' life. On Socrates' commitment to thinking and acting rightly, see the author's essay, "Was Socrates Unwise to Take the Hemlock?" in Harvard Theological Review 65 (1972), 437–52.

6. Derek Bok, "Reflections on the Ethical Problems of Accepting Gifts: An Open Letter to the Harvard Community," in a supplement to the Harvard University Gazette, May 1979, 2–4.

7. "Model Standards of Practice for the Charitable Gift Planner." Available from the National Committee on Planned Giving, 310 N. Alabama St., Suite 210, Indianapolis, IN 46202. In this code, "standard" and "principle" (code provision) are virtually synonymous—a common confusion that can lead one to wrongly assume that the code is self-justifying (see chapter 5). Standards are authoritative, rule-like, and often identify practices and policies of a particular profession, for example accounting practices or academic standards. They need not imply ethical responsibility. However, if they do (as in this code), they become normative assertions that fall well short, as we shall see, of serving as ethical principles.

8. Based on an article by Jeremy Iggers in the Minneapolis–St. Paul Star Tribune, March 6, 1988. In a follow-up article by Doug Grow, April 15, 1994, also of the Star Tribune, the donor was reported as saying the public criticism he endured was unwarranted, a nightmare he describes in his own version, "Framed, Defamed and Destroyed." The donor has continued his questionable mail campaign insisting that his "mission is about respect for life, family and preserving the purity of all races"; moreover, "people have a right to react to my letters any way they want to. They have a right to ignore them or to throw them away. But what about my right? I have a [First Amendment] right to speak up."

9. Jon Pratt, executive director of the Minnesota Council on Nonprofits, in an opinion piece, "Philanthropy's Name Game Goes Too Far," in The Chronicle of Philanthropy, January 25, 1994.

10. See "A Donor Bill of Rights," developed in 1993 by the American Association of Fund Raising Counsel, the Association for Healthcare Philanthropy, the Council for the Advancement and Support of Education, and the National Society of Fund Raising Executives. Endorsed also by other major national organizations this piece has been widely distributed by nonprofits to their donors.

11. Philip Kotler has been most influential; for example, *Principles of Marketing* (Englewood Cliffs: Prentice-Hall, 1980) and contributions to *Cases and Readings for Marketing for Nonprofit Organizations* (Englewood Cliffs: Prentice-Hall, 1983).

12. In a study conducted by the Minnesota Council of Nonprofits, reported in a paper by its executive director, Jon Pratt, "Minnesota Council of Nonprofits Nonprofit Standards Project: Inventing by Consent: Creating a Common Model for Performance," as part of the council's annual conference, October 7, 1993.

13. Andrew Carnegie, *The Gospel of Wealth* (1889), ed. Edward C. Kirkland (Cambridge: Harvard University Press, 1962). See also the essays, particularly the opening historical analysis by Barry D. Karl, collected in *The Responsibilities of Wealth*, to commemorate Carnegie's philanthropic influence.

14. See for example "Tithing," *The New Westminster Dictionary of the Bible*, ed. Henry Snyder Gehman (Philadelphia: Westminster, 1970).

15. The Bible, many versions; for example, *The New English Bible: The New Testament*, second ed. (Oxford: Oxford University Press, Cambridge University Press, 1970).

16. See for example *Fiduciary Duties of Directors of Charitable Organizations* (St. Paul: Charities Division, Attorney General's Office, State of Minnesota, 1993). See also *Council of Better Business Bureaus Standards for Charitable Solicitation* (Washington, DC: Philanthropic Advisory Service, Council of Better Business Bureaus). In a recent dispute with the Minnesota Charities Division, three firefighters organizations and their out-of-state telemarketing firm agreed to a settlement following accusations that the "solicitors represented themselves as local firefighters; failed to say that contributions are not tax-deductible; falsely credited the firefighter groups with playing a significant role in passing an enhanced 911-service bill in the 1993 Legislature; falsely suggested that most of the money raised would be used for charitable purposes, and misrepresented the

percentage that would go to the organizations." As restitution they agreed to buy and distribute some 8,000 smoke detectors for low-income and elderly citizens. See "$60,000 Settles State Telemarketing Case" by Robert Franklin, *Minneapolis–St. Paul Star Tribune* for November 23, 1994.

17. *Ethics and the Nation's Voluntary and Philanthropic Community: Obedience to the Unenforceable*, by the Independent Sector's Committee on Values and Ethics (Washington, DC: Independent Sector, 1991). See also a summary and discussion of it in *The Chronicle of Philanthropy* (hereafter TCP), October 30, 1990. A fine companion manual is available, *Everyday Ethics: Key Ethical Questions for Grantmakers and Grantseekers*, ed. Sandra Trice Gray (Washington, DC: Independent Sector, 1993).

Two   A MATTER OF PRINCIPLE

1. For an excellent review of the history of ethics along with recommended readings, see "Ethics" by Peter Singer in *The New Encyclopaedia Britannica*, vol. 18 of the *Macropaedia*, 15th edition (Chicago: Encyclopaedia Britannica, 1992), 492–521. For in-depth essays on thinkers such as Aristotle, Socrates, Machiavelli, Shaftesbury, Hutcheson, Hume, Locke, Mill, Kant, Kierkegaard, and others, see *The Encyclopedia of Philosophy*, Paul Edwards, editor in chief (New York: Macmillan, Inc. & Free Press; London: Collier Macmillan, 1967). For a first-rate, systematic treatment of ethical frameworks, see Kenneth Goodpaster, "Ethical Frameworks for Management," a case study for Harvard Business School (Boston: Harvard Business School, President and Fellows of Harvard College, 1983). A more recent approach (1994), with the same title but designed as an aid to classroom discussion for management students at St. Thomas University, is noted in note 12 and also referred to in chapter 4.

2. An interesting recent book, *The Moral Sense* (New York: Free Press, 1993), by James Q. Wilson, argues persuasively from studies representing various sciences that despite the prevailing views of contemporary analytical philosophers, who by equating moral judgments with personal preferences have contributed to the moral relativism of our culture, there is an innate moral sense in the human condition. He adduces an impressive amount of evidence to show that when we are not unduly distracted or misled, we

persist as human beings, especially in family settings, in morally judging ourselves and others, and in trying to live by the judgments we make.

3. Alexis de Tocqueville argues that mores or customs are among the most compelling forces to shape American society, in *Democracy in America*, trans. Phillips Bradley (New York: Knopf, 1945), vol. I, chapter XIV.

4. Robert N. Bellah, Richard Madsen, William M. Sullivan, Ann Swidler, and Steven M. Tipton, *Habits of the Heart: Individualism and Commitment in American Life* (New York: Harper & Row, 1985), particularly chapter 3.

5. The view that moral judgments are actually personal preferences was adopted in the twentieth century, for example, by the Logical Positivist movement, which thus placed no confidence in Hume's further notion that there is an innate moral sense in humankind.

6. Niccolo Machiavelli, *The Prince*, introduction, Christian Gauss (New York: Mentor, reprint by Penguin, 1952, from the original by Oxford University Press), especially bks. 14–18.

7. Søren Kierkegaard, *Fear and Trembling*, issued together with *Repetition*, from Kierkegaard's Writings, vol. IV, ed. and trans. Howard V. Hong and Edna H. Hong (Princeton: Princeton University Press, 1983). For comprehensive insight into Kierkegaard's life and authorship, see Reidar Thomte, *Kierkegaard's Philosophy of Religion* (Princeton: Princeton University Press, 1948). On existentialism, see H. J. Blackham, *Six Existentialist Thinkers* (New York: Harper Torchbooks, 1959); old, but among the best essays on the existential views of Kierkegaard, Jaspers, Nietzsche, Marcel, Heidegger, and Sartre.

8. Daniel Callahan, "Minimalist Ethics," *The Hastings Center Report* 11:5, October 1981. Also in *Ethics for Hard Times*, ed. Arthur Caplan and Daniel Callahan (New York: Plenum, 1982).

9. A careful analysis of "egoism" and "altruism" suggests they need not be understood as logically exclusive motives, one (egoism) bad and the other (altruism) good. Rather, as Dwight F. Burlingame argues in "Altruism and Philanthropy: Definitional Issues," in *Essays on Philanthropy, No. 10* (Indianapolis: Indiana University Center on Philanthropy, 1993), 1: "Altruism is one end of a continuum which is anchored by egoism on the other. Both motives come together in the human condition to form a cooperative ven-

ture to achieve nearly all ends in society." Nonetheless, Burlingame notes, these motives can conflict; indeed, "a moral problem surfaces only when the interest of self [egoism] and the interests of others [altruism] conflict," 7.

10. Michael Josephson, founder of the Joseph & Edna Josephson Institute for the Advancement of Ethics, makes trustworthiness one of the six "pillars" of character, along with respect, responsibility, fairness, caring, and citizenship. One of the Institute's surveys revealed an unacceptably high percentage of cheating and lying among young adults. Character development—as Aristotle might agree—is sadly lacking in contemporary American society. Noted in *The Monthly Memo* of the Minnesota Center for Corporate Responsibility, University of St. Thomas, St. Paul, Minnesota, December 1993. The institute also provides resource material for seminars on ethics, and a useful book, *Ethical Issues and Opportunities in the Non-Profit Sector* (Marina del Rey, CA).

11. Romans 7:14–21, where, according to Paul's "principle," the law, such as the Ten Commandments, represents the ultimate ethical standard in relation to which human will and action fail.

12. See the essay, "Ethical Frameworks for Management," Kenneth E. Goodpaster, Koch Professor in Business Ethics, University of St. Thomas, September 1994. The essay was prepared as an aid to classroom discussion and analysis; it may be available by writing to Professor Goodpaster, University of St. Thomas, Minneapolis, MN.

13. John Stuart Mill, *Utilitarianism* (1861), ed. George Sher (Indianapolis: Hackett, 1979).

14. Immanuel Kant, *Foundations of the Metaphysics of Morals* (1785), trans. Lewis White Beck (Indianapolis: Library of Liberal Arts, Bobbs-Merrill, 1959). Perhaps the best modern-day defense of Kantian principles, dubbed "prima facie duties," is by W. D. Ross, *The Right and the Good* (Oxford: Oxford University Press, 1930, reprinted 1973).

15. See Lawrence C. Becker, "Individual Rights," in *And Justice for All*, ed. Tom Regan and Donald VanDeVeer (Totowa, NJ: Rowman & Allenheld, 1983). The breadth of this classification may help one appreciate the ever-widening trend in contemporary American society to claim that one's personal "rights" are being violated in

ways that never would have occurred to us before, and thus to seek redress, often through compensation from the courts, for being "victimized" by others, by society, by government, etc. Observers suggest that it is a tendency to remove the responsibility we once expected to take for our own well-being, and place it—along with the blame for the bumps and bruises of life— on others.

16. For a brilliant critique of Utilitarianism as applied to business and economics, see Alasdair MacIntyre, "Utilitarianism and the Presuppositions of Cost-Benefit Analysis: An Essay on the Relevance of Moral Philosophy to the Theory of Bureaucracy," in *Ethics in Planning*, ed. Martin Wachs (Rutgers, 1985). MacIntyre's book, *After Virtue: A Study in Moral Theory* (Notre Dame: University of Notre Dame Press, second edition, 1984), is a modern-day classic whose challenges, unfortunately, cannot be addressed in this book. The study is an important watershed for examining contemporary moral issues.

17. See also Michael O'Neill, "Fund Raising as an Ethical Act," in *Advancing Philanthropy*, the journal of the National Society of Fund Raising Executives (Fall 1993). A first-rate presentation of ethical lessons applied to fundraising, it also calls on the thought of Aristotle, Kant, and Mill.

Three ISSUES OF CONSEQUENCE AND INTENTION

1. Sydney J. Harris, *Winners & Losers* (Allen, TX: Argus Communications, 1973), 93.

2. I am indebted to my former colleague, Dr. Warren Smerud, Professor of Philosophy, now retired, Concordia College (MN), for this insight.

3. Gilbert Gaul and Neill Boroski, *Free Ride: The Tax-Exempt Economy* (Kansas City: Andrews and McNeel, 1993), particularly chap. 3. Given this nation's constitutional freedoms of speech and religion, one might consider—an extreme case—the potential for abuse in the work of a nonprofit ostensibly dedicated to the charitable and humanitarian support of Muslims, but whose funds are allegedly used to provide the followers of Islamic Jihad and

Hamas with weapons and training in a "holy war," for terrorist activities in this country.

4. See the article by Vince Stehle, "Computer Screening of Donor Lists Enables Many Charities to Zero In on Top Prospects," in TCP, October 31, 1989.

5. In an article by Anne Lowrey Bailey, "Today's Fund-Raising Detectives Hunt 'Suspects' Who Have Big Money to Give," in TCP, June 22, 1988.

6. In an article by Vince Stehle, "Prospect Researchers, Who Collect Confidential Information about Potential Donors, Are Divided over Ethical Questions," from TCP, September 5, 1989.

7. Quoted in *The Chronicle of Higher Education* (hereafter CHE), June 22, 1988.

8. In a story by Dorothy Lewis, "Influence on Will Was Undue, Judge Says," *St. Paul Pioneer Press and Dispatch*, January 14, 1987.

9. "Model Standards of Practice for the Charitable Gift Planner" (see chap. 1, n.7).

10. Douglas E. White, "My View," TCP, March 21, 1989.

11. For a discussion of these issues see Jon Pratt's essay, "What Grant-makers Should Know about Today's Grantseekers," in *The Corporate Contributions Handbook*, ed. James P. Shannon (San Franciso: Jossey-Bass, 1991), 220–22. There are corporate foundations that strongly encourage nonprofits that request funds to involve corporate employees in the project. Presumably the practice serves as added justification to shareholders as well as employees that a portion of the company's profits is well spent as a civic duty, though it might have been distributed as salaries and stock benefits.

12. For a corporate officer's presentation of this issue see Cynthia D. Giroud's essay, "Cause-Related Marketing: Potential Dangers and Benefits," in *The Corporate Contributions Handbook*, 139f. Megan Rosenfeld of the *Washington Post*, reprinted in the *Minneapolis Star Tribune* for May 19, 1994 ("Fine Arts Reluctantly Beginning to Accept Corporate Patrons") notes the quid pro quo arrangements between, for example, the Royal Shakespeare Company and sponsors such as Dunkin' Donuts and Courvoisier cognac who, in return for financing the Company's productions, have exclusive concession and promotion rights to the theatre lobby. Where is the line

crossed between traditional corporate sponsorship of nonprofit programs and for-profit business arrangements? Some corporations now clearly separate their philanthropic contributions from their marketing strategies, though the latter may involve selected nonprofits. For a historical analysis of how corporate grantmaking evolved, see Barry D. Karl's essay, "The Evolution of Corporate Grantmaking in America," in *The Corporate Contributions Handbook*, 2of.

13. Harlan Cleveland, *The Knowledge Executive* (New York: Dutton, 1985), chapter 5, but also chapter 4.

14. A well-known case was reported by Brenton R. Schlender in two articles, "Spreading a Virus," *Wall Street Journal*, November 7, 1988, and "Computer Security Firms Suggest Ways to Stop Viruses," a week later in the same publication. See also the article by John Markoff, "Rogue Computer Program Represents New Technology," *New York Times*, reprinted in the *Minneapolis Star Tribune* for November 10, 1988.

15. See the opinion piece by Priscilla Linsely, "Confessions of an 'Unethical' Fund Raiser," in *TCP*, May 2, 1989; and the article by Kristin Goss and Wendy Melillo, "Vote to End Ban on Commission Payments Stirs Ethics Debate among Fund Raisers," same issue.

16. One of the best discussions is by Gene G. James, "Whistle Blowing: Its Nature and Justification," from *Ethics in Planning*, ed. Martin Wachs (Rutgers: Center for Urban Policy Research, 1985), 162–77; reprinted from *Philosophy in Context* (Cleveland: Cleveland State University Department of Philosophy, 1980), 99–117.

17. Virtually the entire January 1987 issue of *Currents*, the periodical of the Council for Advancement and Support of Education, is devoted to ethical issues for nonprofits, mainly in education.

Four PRINCIPLED ACTION

1. The model also lends itself to a matrix of possible consequences and actions. For a fuller explanation of the model and its application to cases, see Marilyn Fischer, "Ethical Fund Raising: Deciding What's Right," *Advancing Philanthropy*, the Journal of the National Society of Fund Raising Executives, Spring 1994, 29–33.

2. In "Ethical Frameworks for Management," Kenneth E. Goodpaster's paper designed as a classroom aid for management students at St. Thomas University, St. Paul and Minneapolis, Minnesota.

3. See, for example, *Profiles of Excellence: Achieving Success in the Nonprofit Sector*, by E. B. Knauft, Renee Berger, and Sandra T. Gray (San Francisco: Jossey-Bass, 1991).

Five A PRACTITIONER'S CODE OF ETHICS

1. Two articles in the May 25, 1987 issue of *Time* document the ethical improprieties of top government and business leaders during the mid-1980s: "Morality among the Supply-Siders," by Richard Stengel, reported by David Beckwith, 18–20, notes cases alleging serious ethics violations representing over 100 Reagan era officials. Stengel concludes: "one of the sad commentaries . . . is that so many of those tainted . . . still seem unable to divine what was wrong with their concept of government service"; also, "Having It All, Then Throwing It All Away," by Stephen Koepp, reported by Harry Kelly and Rajl Samghabadl, 22–23, describes a rash of white-collar crimes among high-level executives, including insider trading, money laundering, and greenmail motivated by greed combined with technology, and the pressure to perform.

2. Harlan Cleveland, *The Future Executive* (New York: Harper & Row, 1972), 104. Chapters 8 and 9 are excellent essays on the topic of moral leadership for public executives.

3. Many versions; for example *The Republic of Plato* trans. Francis M. Cornford (Oxford: Oxford University Press, 1945), chapter 5, p. 44f.

4. "Stealing from the Hand That Feeds You," by Ann Merrill, staff writer for the *Minneapolis Star Tribune*, October 3, 1994.

5. The code for the Council for the Advancement and Support of Education is available from the council's offices, 11 Dupont Circle, Suite 400, Washington, DC, 20036. See also *CASE CAMPAIGN STANDARDS*, available from CASE Publications Order Department.

6. Quoted by Kristin A. Goss in "Internal Misconduct Leads Nonprofits to Look to Their Missions to Resolve Ethical Questions," TCP, July 2, 1991.

7. In addition to Cleveland's books, see Robert Terry, *Authentic Leadership: Courage in Action* (San Francisco: Jossey-Bass, 1993). For a perti-

nent and perceptive analysis of the corporate grantmaking milieu
and of the "styles" of leadership one finds in it, see the essay by
James P. Shannon, a distinguished veteran of corporate philanthropy, "Successful Corporate Grantmaking: Lessons to Build
On," in *The Corporate Contributions Handbook*, ed. James P. Shannon
(San Francisco: Jossey-Bass, 1991), 343–46 and in Resource C of
the same, 374f., an excerpt from Independent Sector's "Profiles of
Effective Corporate Giving Programs." Styles include: the loyal sol-
dier, the skillful tactician, the change agent, the broker-advocate,
and the technocrat.

8. See "Ethical Leadership" by George Shapiro, a professor at the
University of Minnesota, in *Focus*, a publication of the University
of Minnesota Office of Educational Development Programs, vol.
IV, no. 1, Fall 1988.

9. A discussion of current views of corporate responsibility is presented by Jeremy Iggers, "How Should Companies Behave?," in
the *Minneapolis Star Tribune* for April 18, 1994. As an ongoing forum
for discussing these issues, see *Business Ethics*, a first-rate magazine
that has as its mission "to promote ethical business practices, to
serve that growing community of professionals striving to live
and work in responsible ways, and to create a financially healthy
company in the process." Kenneth E. Goodpaster has written a
very helpful essay, "The Concept of Corporate Responsibility," in
Just Business: New Essays in Business Ethics, ed. Tom Regan (New York:
Random, 1984). An article by John J. Oslund of the *Minneapolis Star
Tribune* for May 19, 1994, "Chinese Puzzle: Minnesotan Has Idea
for Dealing with Trade Dilemma: A Code of Conduct," notes a
proposal by Robert MacGregor, president of the Minnesota Center
for Corporate Responsibility, urging corporations that do business
in China to adopt a code of conduct similar to the Sullivan Principles adopted by major firms such as 3M to ameliorate apartheid
in South Africa. The proposed China code would allow ongoing
business while making various efforts to address human rights issues; in general, international business should be characterized by
fairness, honesty, respect for human dignity, and respect for the
environment, applied to all stakeholders.

10. The Johnson & Johnson code is succinctly written as "Our
Credo"; American Can Company's code is a well-developed man-
ual; the Levi Strauss & Co.'s position is brief and to the point: six
"Ethical Principles" and a "Code of Ethics" based on four "val-

ues." Robert Dunn, Strauss's foundation executive, has coauthored with Judith Babbitts the essay "Being Ethical and Accountable in the Grantmaking Process," *The Corporate Contributions Handbook*. For an in-depth examination of the philosophies, policies, and procedures of ten major corporations, including Johnson & Johnson, see *Corporate Ethics: A Prime Business Asset* (New York: Business Roundtable, 1988).

11. "Mission And Values: Stanford University Office of Development," Henry E. Riggs, vice president for development.

12. The manual, *Everyday Ethics*, ed. Sandra Trice Gray (Washington, DC: Independent Sector, 1993), offers nonprofit organizations a list of "key ethical questions" by which to measure themselves against the recommendations of the Independent Sector study. The questions quoted are from page 4, under the heading "Commitment Beyond the Law."

Index

agement of, 113, 122, 127–29. See also donors

integrity. See professionalism

intentions, 7–9, 40–42, 100; consequences and, 46–48; ethics and, 9–13, 136n.8; philanthropic, 124. See also charitable intent

interests, public and private, 105

intrusiveness, 54–57, 63–64, 112

Jesus, 15–17, 60, 116

Johnson & Johnson: "Our Credo," 106–107, 129–30

justice: Aristotle on, 9

Kant, Immanuel, xi, xii–xiii, 29, 32, 33–34, 35, 38, 40–42, 43–44, 47

Kierkegaard, Søren, 34, 35, 47; Fear and Trembling, 30, 34–35

Knowledge Executive, The (Cleveland), 64

laws, compliance with, 26–27, 121, 126, 129

leap of faith, 47

Levi Strauss & Co.: Ethical Principles, 106–107, 129–32

list-selling, 53, 119, 122

Locke, John, 35, 42

Machiavelli, Niccolo: The Prince, 30

Malachi, 16

marketing: cause-related, 61–62, 95–96, 142n.11; prospects and, 55

Mill, John Stuart, xi, xii–xiii, 6, 34, 35, 38, 47; on goodness, 39–40, 43

"Model Standards of Practice for the Charitable Gift Planner" (National Committee on Planned Giving), 9, 124–27, 136n.7

moderation, 4, 5–6, 23–24

moral sense, 25, 29, 138n.2, 139n.5

morality, 23–25, 28–29, 116–17; ethics and, 26, 31; the law and, 26–27, 121, 126, 129; relativism of, ix–x, 24, 27–28, 29, 31, 45, 139n.5. See also ethics

motives. See intentions

Moulton, John Fletcher, 19

National Committee on Planned Giving: "Model Standards of Practice for the Charitable Gift Planner," 9, 59–60, 124–27, 136n.7

National Society of Fund Raising Execu-

tives, 76–77; Codes of Ethical Principles and Standards of Professional Practice, 65, 120–22

Nichomachean Ethics (Aristotle), 1, 104

non-consequentialism. See formalism

nonprofits, 18, 77, 111, 137n.16; abuse by, 51–52, 141n.3; charitable intent and, 60–61, 67; codes of ethics for, 18–22; conflict of interest and, 62–63, 142nn.11,12; divulging donor/prospect information, 53–54; donors' private affairs and, 54–57; ethical action and, 115–18; ethics and, 11–13; exploiting relationships, 57–60, 67, 119; gagging whistle-blowers, 68–69; misuse of donor funds, 52–53, 118; questionable expenses, 65–68; records and, 64–65; security and, 63–64

nothing in excess. See moderation

O'Neill, Michael, 103

"Open Letter, An" (Bok), 8–9

ought, morality and, 25–26, 31; ought vs. is, 29

"Our Credo" (Johnson & Johnson), 106–107, 129–30

Paul, the apostle, 36

philanthropists, 13–15

philanthropy, 1, 5, 8, 9, 12–13, 68, 73, 75, 115–16, 119, 124, 135n.2; ethics of, 13–15; Jesus and, 15–17. See also codes of ethics

planned giving, 59

Plato: The Republic, 100–101

Prince, The (Machiavelli), 30

principles, ethical, 36–37, 44–45, 110–11, 117, 127–28. See also beneficence; formalism; respect; trust; utilitarianism

privacy, 54–57, 63–64, 74, 97–98, 111, 118; codes of ethics on, 121, 122, 123, 127, 129, 133

professionalism, 1–5, 56–57, 65, 125–26, 131, 133

promise-keeping, 75, 85, 131

prospects, 54–55; as suspect, 55–57

public interest, 105

public trust, 19, 111, 126–27

purpose, fidelity of, 75, 80, 85, 118

quid pro quo arrangements, 10–11

reason, practical, 23, 33

regulation, nonprofits and, 105–106, 112

Albert Anderson has over twenty-five years of experience at executive levels of management and development in private and public higher education. He has served as vice president for planning/administration at the University of Minnesota Foundation, and as consultant to a broad range of nonprofit and government organizations. Currently he is serving as consultant to and President of College Misericordia in Dallas, Pennsylvania; previously, he served for nearly seven years as President of Lenoir Rhyne College in Hickory, North Carolina. He has published in *The Harvard Theological Review* and *The Review of Metaphysics*, and is a contributor to *The Responsibilities of Wealth*.